THE MONTREAL CANADIENS

Rethinking a Legend

One of the most famous and successful professional hockey teams of all time, the Montreal Canadiens are a major institution in Quebec society. Perhaps more than any other team in Canada, the Habs are integral to the identity, economy, and culture of their home town and province.

The essays in *The Montreal Canadiens: Rethinking a Legend* delve into the causes and effects of the team's extraordinary influence. What were the connections between the Maurice Richard Riot of 1955 and Quebec's Quiet Revolution? Can we say that loyalty to the team constitutes a religion for its fans? How is corporatization affecting how Quebecers connect with their beloved team? Featuring a wide range of perspectives on Le Grand Club and its social significance, the book offers a fresh and fascinating take on one of Canada's greatest sports teams.

NICOLAS MOREAU is an associate professor in the School of Social Work at the University of Ottawa.

AUDREY LAURIN-LAMOTHE is a doctoral candidate in the Department of Sociology at l'Université du Québec à Montréal.

MARIE-PIER RIVEST is a doctoral candidate in the School of Social Work at the University of Ottawa.

THE MONTREAL CANADIENS

Rethinking a Legend

Edited by Nicolas Moreau and
Audrey Laurin-Lamothe
with Marie-Pier Rivest

Translated by Howard Scott

UNIVERSITY OF TORONTO PRESS
Toronto Buffalo London

Toronto Buffalo London
www.utppublishing.com
Printed in the U.S.A.

ISBN 978-1-4426-4869-2 (cloth)
ISBN 978-1-4426-2633-1 (paper)

Printed on acid-free, 100% post-consumer recycled paper with vegetable-based inks.

Library and Archives Canada Cataloguing in Publication

Canadien de Montréal. English
The Montreal Canadiens : rethinking a legend / edited by Nicolas Moreau and Audrey Laurin-Lamothe ; with Marie-Pier Rivest ; translated by Howard Scott.

Translation of: Le Canadien de Montréal, une legende repensée.
Includes bibliographical references.
ISBN 978-1-4426-4869-2 (bound).—ISBN 978-1-4426-2633-1 (paperback)

1. Montreal Canadiens (Hockey team). 2. Hockey–Social aspects–Québec (Province). 3. Hockey fans–Québec (Province). 4. Hockey players–Québec (Province). I. Moreau, Nicolas, 1977–, editor II. Laurin-Lamothe, Audrey, editor III. Title.

GV848.M6C3613 2015 796.962'640971428 C2015-904035-3

University of Toronto Press acknowledges the financial assistance to its publishing program of the Canada Council for the Arts and the Ontario Arts Council, an agency of the Government of Ontario.

Canada Council for the Arts | Conseil des Arts du Canada

ONTARIO ARTS COUNCIL
CONSEIL DES ARTS DE L'ONTARIO
an Ontario government agency
un organisme du gouvernement de l'Ontario

Funded by the Government of Canada | Financé par le gouvernement du Canada

Canada

Contents

THE MONTREAL CANADIENS

Rethinking a Legend

Introduction: The Montreal Canadiens as a Social Fact

AUDREY LAURIN-LAMOTHE, NICOLAS MOREAU, AND MARIE-PIER RIVEST

It is common to think of hockey in general and the Montreal Canadiens in particular as a unifying factor in Quebec society. One way to appreciate the importance of this team is to measure the space it occupies in the news media. According to Influence Communication, in 2013, over a period of seven days, the Montreal Canadiens occupied five of the top fifty places as most quoted by traditional news media (i.e., outside the Internet).[1] In 2011, twelve of the twenty-five personalities (in general) receiving the most media coverage in Quebec, and eight of the ten sports personalities, belonged to Le Grand Club. When you talk about sports in Quebec, you talk mostly about hockey, and especially about the Habs, since the team accounts for 78 per cent of sportscasts. Media coverage of the Montreal Canadiens in La Belle Province represented 12 per cent of all news in 2013. Again according to Influence Communication, the Montreal Canadiens ranked third, after general news and provincial politics.

It seems imperative to examine this enthusiasm for the Montreal Canadiens in terms of its social significance. Émile Durkheim would say that Le Grand Club is a *social fact* – that is, a collective phenomenon that exists in its own right "independently of individuals' wills" and that exercises over individuals a substantial form of constraint (Durkheim, 1982). The Habs are the site of a consolidation of history, identity, economics, and culture. To borrow the slogan of the team's centenary, history indeed plays here, when we consider Le Grand Club in its social context. This book explores these interpretative avenues and suggests various ways of examining the connections that exist between Quebec society and the Habs. English Canadian readers will thus be able to compare their own experiences of that sport with those of Quebecers.

They will see how similar analyses could be done in Canada, and they will be able to examine the example of the Montreal Canadiens as a link between society and a professional hockey team. Le Grand Club is one of the "original six" teams in the National Hockey League (NHL), and it has achieved mythic status in the sport because of its history and its unrivalled record (twenty-four Stanley Cups), just as the New York Yankees have done in baseball. For readers who are passionate soccer fans, a similar comparison is possible in terms of the sport/society dialectic, given that some major European clubs (FC Barcelona, Juventus of Turin, Manchester United, Liverpool, etc.) are part of the identity of their cities (Bromberger, 1995).

Although this is changing, traditionally there have been two types of literature on sports and athletes. First, there are hagiographies of athletes, in which the subjects are presented as idols, models, heroes, myths. According to some, this allows the expression of a democratic ideal, however constantly that ideal is flouted in reality (Ehrenberg, 1991). An example is Maurice Richard, who, through his excellence, advanced the cause of the French Canadian nation at a time when it was under the English Canadian yoke. There have been many books about Richard, as well as biographies of Jean Béliveau, Jacques Plante, Guy Lafleur, and others. Second, there is sports literature that focuses on scandal, exposing all of the abuses common in the world of sports (doping, financial shenanigans, cheating) that are constantly tarnishing the mythical ideal represented by its heroes (Thomazeau, 2014; Ballester, 2013). As pointed out by Fleuriel and Schotté, "the alternation between euphoric exaltation of athletic competition and pure denunciation of its misdeeds delimits the range of the thinkable" (2008, p. 6; translation).

Fortunately, some books have broken through this impasse and opened the way for a thorough analysis of hockey and the Montreal Canadiens, both in English Canada and in Quebec. We would mention first of all the popular documentary series produced by the CBC in 2006, *Hockey: A People's History*, in which hockey was presented as the national winter sport through a telling of its history and that of its main Canadian protagonists. That series had the merit of examining hockey in general – in other words, it dealt with the sport beyond its strictly professional framework. It was not just about NHL players, but about women's and amateur hockey as well.

On a more academic register, two books by Gruneau and Whitson are essential reading for those who want to understand hockey as both a popular activity and an industry. In *Hockey Night in Canada: Sport, Identities, and Cultural Politics* (1993), the authors examine the national and mythical dimensions of hockey – that is, hockey as a romantic mixture of truths and omissions. Their deconstruction of the hockey myth can be viewed as oppositional to the CBC documentary, which made hockey one of Canada's principal unifying factors.

In *Artificial Ice: Hockey, Culture, and Commerce* (2006), the same authors invite us to question the economic aspects of hockey. With an approach that is just as critical as in their first book, they examine the economic development of the NHL and its impact on social representations of the sport. Fans of professional hockey have watched the sport change before their eyes, and they are sometimes bitter about it.

Similar themes of marketing and culture are encountered in *Canada's Game: Hockey and Identity* (2009), edited by Andrew C. Holman. This book explores questions of Canadian identity through an analysis of films and other cultural materials about the sport.

In 2001, Michael A. Robidoux published *Men at Play: A Working Understanding of Professional Hockey*, based on his ethnographic research on the American Hockey League. Having observed games, the interactions between players, and their informal activities, he was able to throw light on various dimensions of their world. Homophobia, violence, and degrading initiations were part of the daily lives of these players.

In *Refereeing Identity: The Cultural Work of Canadian Hockey Novels* (2012), Michael Buma has analysed hockey's innately masculine identity. Works of fiction have long constructed and disseminated the perception that hockey is a rough, virile sport; today, fictional works are questioning that perception. John Chi-Kit Wong's *Lords of the Rinks: The Emergence of the National Hockey League* (2005) examines how hockey has been marketed since the sport's beginnings. Wong is also the editor of *Coast to Coast: Hockey in Canada to the Second World War*, which posits that the sport does not in fact define a unified national identity (cf. the vision presented in the above-mentioned CBC documentary); rather, its meaning for Canadians varies with their sociodemographic and ethnic origins, gender and place of residence.

Among French-language works, two books by Marc Lavoie on the economics of hockey, *Avantage numérique: L'argent et la Ligue nationale de hockey* (1997a), and *Désavantage numérique: Les francophones dans la LNH* (1997b), ask a number of questions raised every day by journalists as well as by fans: Is hockey being Americanized? Is hockey violence profitable? Was the departure of the Nordiques from Quebec City an economic catastrophe for the city?

With regard more specifically to the Montreal Canadiens, four books deserve special mention. Benoît Melançon's *Les yeux de Maurice Richard* (2006) examines the influence of heroes in Quebec and Canadian society. How did this man become a national hero? Melançon attempts to answer this question by examining the various social representations of Richard over the years – sports writing, biographies, scholarly articles, photographs, songs, plays, poems, clothes, effigies. Through an analysis of these, Melançon summarizes the major trends that made possible the creation of a mythic figure. In *Habitants et Glorieux: Les Canadiens de 1909 à 1960* (1997), the historian François Black takes us from the birth of the Habs to the beginning of their glory days, showing us the events that led to the team becoming a national icon.

In *La religion du Canadien de Montréal* (2009), Olivier Bauer and Jean-Marc Barreau feed the debate over the place of Le Grand Club in the Quebec imaginary and examine the connection between religion and hockey. Finally, *La rivalité Canadien–Nordiques* (2011) by Steve Lasorsa analyses a sports rivalry in the context of nationalism and the Quebec sovereignty referendums of 1980 and 1995.

Rather than adding to the myth of the Montreal Canadiens, our objective is to suggest perspectives for reflection that will permit both sports fans and academics to deepen and broaden their knowledge of the Montreal Canadiens. Like the books mentioned above, this volume takes a position in favour of studies of popular culture. Too often, it seems, intellectuals are seen as snobs who disdain hockey. They are not, and as the books mentioned above suggest, the humanities and social sciences could do much to further our understanding of the Canadiens as a cultural phenomenon.

Our project was born out of a conference titled "100 ans de polysémie. Regards et réflexions sur les Canadiens de Montréal," held in Ottawa in May 2009 as part of the annual conference of the Association francophone pour le savoir (ACFAS). The contributors offer a range of perspectives – from economics to philosophy, sociology, urban planning, and religious studies – that open the way for a critical, reflexive examination of Le Grand Club, perspectives that, six years after their first formulation and four years after the publication of the French-language book (Laurin-Lamothe and Moreau, 2011), remain highly relevant.

This book opens with a key moment in the history of Quebec: the riot that took place in downtown Montreal in 1955. The article by Suzanne Laberge illustrates the potential an athlete has as a social actor – in this case as a symbol of French Canadian identity. The Richard/Campbell affair spilled over considerably into the political dimension and probably served as a catalyst for the liberation of French Canadians. It marked the beginning of a series of collective actions against the omnipresence of the Catholic religion and would lead to what was later called the Quiet Revolution. While the role of religion has significantly diminished in Quebec public life, private life abounds in rituals and beliefs that are sometimes orchestrated explicitly, which suggests that religion is not a thing of the past. This is the idea put forward in chapter 2 by Olivier Bauer in the parallel he draws between religion and the Montreal Canadiens, by presenting practices by fans that have all the characteristics of religious acts.

Dissecting articles on Le Grand Club published in the Montreal daily *La Presse* during the 2010 playoffs, Nicolas Moreau and Chloé Nahas in chapter 3 analyse the qualities attributed to players on the Montreal Canadiens (or demanded of them) in order to better understand contemporary social norms – in other words, what is implicitly and explicitly required of individuals. Here, hockey is understood as revealing characteristics of contemporary Western society, as a normative laboratory.

Chapter 4 by Fannie Valois-Nadeau is based on discourse analysis, but here she looks at the fans as they express themselves through the discussion forum Réseau des sports (RDS). A cultural studies perspective has led her to view the moment of reception of the cultural object as worthy of scholarly interest. For example, Valois-Nadeau finds that the fans are constantly negotiating the representation of the Canadiens put to them by the media and by the corporation itself. The Canadiens in this way become a place to express society's conflicts and contradictions, whether these arise from tensions in marketing, in national identity, or in tradition.

The next chapters address hockey marketing. Audrey Laurin-Lamothe in chapter 5 discusses the corporate nature of the Canadiens, examining the club's origins, its ethnolinguistic make-up, and its business strategies. She points out the organization's major changes over time in how it presents of itself and in its relationship with the public. She notes the emergence over the past three decades of a brand that has been imposed as an unescapable cultural agent on the Quebec landscape.

The corporation's expansion into the social fabric is also evident in terms of urban planning. In this context, we have seen emerge in Montreal a strong partnership between the municipality and the club. Jonathan Cha in chapter 6 systematizes the undertaking pursued by the actors in that synergy and sees in it the conquest by hockey of the urban space.

Finally, in chapter 7, on a more philosophical note, Alain Deneault examines fandom, its authenticity, and its deleterious impact on social bonds. The shedding of inhibitions by euphoric fans leads him to ask who benefits from fandom. Politics and sport are, according to him, inextricably linked in an alienating process that we should examine more closely.

The authors of this collection address various themes but share the common objective of highlighting the place occupied by the Habs on the Quebec social stage, thus elucidating the multiple relationships that can be established between sport and society (Moreau, 2008).

NOTE

1 These data are taken from the Influence Communication report, *État de la nouvelle: Bilan, 2013*. Québec.

1 The Richard/Campbell Affair: Hockey as the Catalyst for Quebec Francophone Affirmation[1]

SUZANNE LABERGE

The state funeral, the popular demonstrations of admiration and sadness, and the media coverage around the death of Maurice Richard (27 May 2000) bore witness to his symbolic weight not only in the sporting world but also in Quebec and Canadian society. As is often the case with heroes, each nation or social group to which the heroic figure can be associated appropriates him as *its* symbol. To what nation does the mythical figure of the "Rocket" belong? To Quebec, to French Canada, to all of Canada ... or quite simply to hockey? On the basis of testimony and comments from fans of various allegiances in newspapers and the electronic media after the death of Maurice Richard, we could say that he belongs to all of these.

For Lawrence Martin in the *Ottawa Citizen*, Richard was a Canadian symbol comparable to Pierre Elliott Trudeau: "Richard takes on more meaning, more value to Canada than that of a great hockey player. In his passing he has become a cultural giant, an endless source of a most precious national product: patriotism" (1 June 2000). Conversely, for Jean-Luc Duguay in *Le Devoir*, he was the emblem of French Canadians: "It was the little guy from the working-class neighbourhood who made his way in the world of the big guys and thumbed his nose at the English Canadian players. He was more than an idol. He had become an icon, a sacred image that could not be touched" (30 May 2000; translation). The online version of the *National Post*, for its part, opted for hockey: "But these political passions should not figure prominently in our remembrance of the Rocket, for he never lent his name or stature to their advancement. He was first and foremost a hockey player, and he should be remembered as such" (31 May 2000).

The riot of 17 March 1955, in reaction to Richard's suspension by Clarence Campbell, the NHL president, strongly attests to Richard's social and political influence on French Canadians in the postwar years. For some commentators, this incident "marked a major turning point in the evolution of Quebec society, awakening nationalist pride" (*Le Devoir*, 29 May 2000; translation); for others, that is a misleading interpretation by the Quebec nationalist intelligentsia, for the Rocket was "apolitical." We can cite, for example, articles by William Houston ("No place for Politicians," *The Globe and Mail*, 1 June 2000) and Matthew Fisher ("The Rocket Played Hockey, Not Politics," *Toronto Sun*, 2 June 2000). An article in the *Calgary Herald* even claimed that the Rocket would never have touched the passionate debate on sovereignty "even with a 10-foot pole" (quoted in *Le Devoir*, 5 June 2000, p. A6).

We want here to highlight various elements that point to the mobilizing power and symbolic significance of the Rocket with French Canadians of the time. Specifically, we will attempt to show that the Richard/Campbell affair acted as a catalyst in the movement for national affirmation. Our analysis is based on the events and comments reported from 17 to 25 March 1955 in four French newspapers (*La Presse, Le Montréal-Matin, Le Devoir, La Patrie*) – and four English newspapers (*Montreal Star, Globe and Mail, The Gazette, The Herald*)[2] as well as in the archival documents and the interviews shown in the film *Mon frère Richard* by Luc Cyr and Carl Leblanc (Ad Hoc films, 1999) and the television series *Maurice Richard* (SRC, 1999).

The Symbolic Power of Maurice Richard: A "Typical French Canadian" and a Champion

To better understand the social impact of the Richard/Campbell affair, we must first recall certain character traits. On the one hand, Maurice Richard's symbolic force is based on the fact that in many ways he embodied the typical French Canadian of the 1950s: the oldest of eight children in a working-class family, he was relatively uneducated (he had taken classes at a technical school to become a machinist); like his father, he was a worker at an English Canadian company (the Canadian Pacific Railway); and he was a unilingual francophone. He was married, the father of a small family, and a practising Catholic. Finally, he was determined to win at hockey through effort and perseverance – personal qualities promoted by the Catholic religion. In all of this, he epitomized the "little people" of Quebec society. His drawing power with francophones was also based on his extraordinary athletic gifts. At the time of the Richard/Campbell affair, Richard was an NHL superstar. He was, for example, the first player to score four hundred goals. *Maclean's* in 1951 called him "Hockey's Greatest Scoring Machine," and *Sports Illustrated* in 1954 published a laudatory feature about him that noted the particular admiration French Canadians had for him, as shown by the following excerpt:

> For 10 years now because of his courage, his skill, and that magical uncultivatable quality, true magnetism, Maurice Richard has reigned in Montreal and throughout the province of Quebec as a hero whose hold on the public has no parallel in sport today unless it be the country-wide adoration that the people of Spain have from time to time heaped on their rare master matadors. The fact that 75 per cent of the citizens of Montreal and a similar percentage of the Forum regulars are warm-blooded, excitable French-Canadians – and what is more, a hero-hungry people who think of themselves not as the majority group in their province but as the minority group in Canada – goes quite a distance in explaining their idolatry of Richard. "If Maurice were an English-Canadian or a Scottish-Canadian or a kid from the West he would be lionized, but not as much as he is now," an English-Canadian Richard follower declared last month. "I go to all the games with a French-Canadian friend of mine, a fellow named Roger Ouellette. I know exactly what Roger thinks. He accepts the English as good as anyone. But he would hate to see the French population lose their language and their heritage generally. He doesn't like the fact that the government's pension checks are printed only in English. He feels that they should be printed in both English and French since the constitution of the Dominion provides for a two-language country. For Roger, Maurice Richard personifies French Canada and all that is great about it. Maybe you have to have French blood, really, to worship Richard, but you know, you only have to be a lover of hockey to admire him." (Wind, 1954)

In short, Richard represented not only someone with whom people from the "little" French Canadian nation could identify, but also a figure who commanded boundless admiration for his athletic exploits. He epitomized the French Canadian who had "succeeded," who was "better than the English." He therefore possessed the qualities required to become a model – and possibly a mobilizing symbol – for French Canadians.

One Distinctive Trait: The Affirmation of His National Pride

At that time, it was rare for an uneducated worker to publicly express his national pride. Such political action was more the prerogative of the French Canadian elite. However, Richard stood out because of his public manifestations of national pride and his denunciations of anglophone domination in the field of sport. In fact, the Maurice Richard of the 1950s was far from the apolitical personality that some contemporary commentators talked about.

For one thing, he was associated with the beginnings of the nationalist movement, having participated, in 1952 and in 1956, in the election campaigns of Maurice Duplessis, the leader of the Union Nationale and one of the first Quebec politicians to promote the affirmation of Quebec within Confederation (Black, 1977).[3] Also, he used his sports column "Le tour du Chapeau" (the hat trick) in the weekly *Samedi-Dimanche* to express, when the opportunity presented itself, either his pride in being French Canadian or his disgust with certain behaviours by anglophone sporting officials whom he saw as discriminating against French Canadian players.[4]

With respect to his nationalism, we can quote, for example, the two following excerpts: "It is the cause of the Canadiens and the prestige of French Canadian athletes that I care about most after that of my little family"; "People should not, however, accuse me of losing my French feelings or let me get dazzled by the English influence of the continent. I still remain 'canayen' as Georges Vézina's tuque and québécois above all."[5] Note, by the way, that the term "québécois," with its nationalist connotations, was just beginning to be used then.

As for the NHL governors' bias against French Canadians, his column of 3 January 1954 denounced it so strongly that he received very severe reprimands. Considering the punishment imposed on Bernard Geoffrion to be profoundly unjust and discriminatory, Richard called the referee Chadwick a "mange-canayen" ("canayen eater")[6] and Clarence Campbell a "dictateur" who was prejudiced against French Canadians:

> Mr. Campbell should not try to promote himself by going after a good guy like "Boom-Boom" Geoffrion, *simply because he is French Canadian!* I have the impression that Mr. Campbell is *biased*. His whole way of acting seems to prove it, and because of that the Canadiens club suffers more than any other team in the National League. That is my honest opinion and if that brings me sanctions, well, that's just too bad! I will leave hockey and I have an idea that many other players in the Canadiens who share my opinion will do the same thing! But there has to be change somewhere![7]

Through his blunt outspokenness, Richard was the antithesis of the "pissou."[8] During the 1950s, his words and his actions helped make him the icon of a French Canadian who was not afraid to affirm his identity or to denounce anglophone oppression. That trait would play a decisive role in the mobilization of French Canadians to affirm their national identity.

Public Repression: Censorship of the Column

The response of the English-speaking sports authorities would help make Richard a symbolic "victim of English oppression." Judging Richard's criticisms unacceptable, the NHL governors pressured him to publicly apologize and stop writing his column. On 16 January 1954, *Samedi-Dimanche* ran an uppercase headline on its front page: "Richard is Gagged." The Rocket wrote in his column:

> This is my last column as a journalist. I regret it, because I found a certain pleasure in expressing my personal opinions on things related to hockey.
>
> *I am being refused that right. I no longer have freedom of speech.* As a hockey player, I am *obliged to obey the orders of my employers.* I am not judging their decision. I will instead let my friends judge it. Perhaps later, *when I don't have my hands tied behind my back,* I will come back.[9]

Thus, even as he resigned his column, Richard continued to denounce the abuse of power by "his employers." He was not the first player to question Campbell's decisions,[10] but his criticisms were probably perceived as more damning because they raised the question of ethnic relations. The repression by anglophone sports officials went beyond the realm of sports and would exacerbate the relationships between the two communities. For French Canadians, Richard was being attacked because he had had the audacity to denounce the ethnic bias of a decision. The oppressed now identified even more with their scorned hero. All of this would reinforce the image of Richard as a victim of the "English" and trigger an unprecedented ethnic and popular mobilization.

The Richard/Campbell Affair

The Crime and the Punishment: The Crystallization of Ethnic Relations

To get a full understanding of the impact of the riot of 17 March 1955, it is important to recall briefly the triggering events of 13 March. During a late-season game against the Boston Bruins, Richard struck an opposing player, Hal Laycoe, who had just hit him with his stick, giving him a deep cut in the head. In the ensuing brawl, Richard punched a linesman who was trying to restrain him. The referee gave Richard a match penalty for attempting to injure Laycoe, and gave Laycoe five minutes for hitting Richard on the head. Because of the seriousness of the incident, the league president, Clarence Campbell, was required to investigate and decide on appropriate further sanctions.

Following a meeting in New York City with the NHL governors, who had already expressed their irritation with what they viewed as Richard's "hot-headed temper" (Duperreault, 1981, pp. 72–74), Campbell opted to make an example of him. In a press release – issued only in English, as usual[11] – he announced that he was suspending Richard until the end of the season, including the playoffs, and that he would no longer tolerate Richard's actions: "The time for probation or leniency is past. Whether this type of conduct is the product of temperamental instability or wilful defiance of the authority in the game does not matter. It is a type of conduct which cannot be tolerated from any player – star or otherwise" (quoted by O'Brien, 1961, pp. 72–74). This decision would crystallize the social representation of Campbell as an "English oppressor" and that of Richard as a "French Canadian victim of discrimination." To understand the impact of the punishment, recall that it meant Richard was being denied the scoring title he was close to achieving and that had eluded him until then, and that for the Canadiens as a team, it would now be nearly impossible for them to win the Stanley Cup, with everything that entailed in terms of honour and prestige. Note also that the Canadiens symbolized francophones in a way, for the team roster included six of the twelve francophone players then active in the NHL.

Genesis of the Political Event: The Progressive Rise of the Revolt

In another context, the punishment given to Maurice Richard would have had consequences only for hockey. But in the context of Quebec in 1955, it would generate a *political event* in the sense used by Fecteau – that is, it would be an event "in which all the dimensions that make up social existence are condensed" and through which is produced a "split" in the social space and the social order of dominant/dominated relationships (1998; translation). The sanction imposed by Clarence Campbell would disrupt the quiet resignation of French Canadians and give rise to a collective movement of indignation, an emotional and social revolt that was politically charged.

Public discontent manifested itself in radio broadcasts and in newspapers and quickly snowballed. Pellerin (1998, p. 307) reports that a telegram of support signed by more than 5,000 fans from the Saguenay region was sent to Richard. Katz reported that Campbell had received hundreds of threatening letters from Richard's supporters, some of whom denounced ethnic discrimination. Two examples: "If Richard's name was Richardson you would have given a different verdict"; "You're just another Englishman jealous of the French, who are much better than you" (1955). Marcel Desmarais, a rioter interviewed by Cyr and Leblanc (1999; translation), recalls: "Being suspended by that English guy, you know ... I found that he had given a sledge hammer blow to French Canadians when he did that." It seems that in the eyes of French Canadians, Campbell was punishing not just a hockey player but the entire French Canadian community.

The response to Richard's punishment highlighted the linguistic split in the sanction's symbolic impact: anglophone newspapers emphasized Richard's unacceptable violence on the ice and Campbell's necessary firmness,[12] while the French-language newspapers unanimously denounced Campbell's unwarranted severity and the ethnic discrimination it demonstrated.

Here are a few illustrations from the anglophone press. The *Globe and Mail* ran the headline "Richard Is Lucky He Didn't Get Life, Said Ted Lindsay" (17 March 1955, p. 31), and its sports editorialist Gord Walker wrote: "Clarence Campbell will be vilified and abused in Montreal for the disciplinary action he took against Rocket Richard yesterday. In Detroit, Boston and all points north, south, east and west, he will be commended for the same performance of duty ... Richard is a menace to the physical well-being of every rival in the NHL." In Montreal, the *Gazette* reported the words of Conn Smythe of the Toronto Maple Leafs: "Our own players know what the rules are and they conform to them, and so do nearly all the other players in the league, and the suspension of Richard will protect the players in the future" (18 March, p. 24). The *Montreal Star* quoted what it called the "impartial" view of Frank Ahearn: "I was deeply impressed by Clarence Campbell's courageous and justified finding in the Richard case" (17 March, p. 45).

Meanwhile, the French-language newspapers contrasted the reactions of anglophones and francophones, denounced Campbell's severity, and called Richard a victim of injustice. *La Patrie* ran this headline on the front page of its 17 March edition: "Richard's Suspension. Campbell Receives Death Threats. Decision Sparks Violent Protests" (translation). Jacques Beauchamp of the *Montréal-Matin* titled his column "Victim of a New Injustice, the Worst This Time, Maurice Richard Will Play No More This Season" and continued in the same issue with "Glaring Injustice of Clarence Campbell" (17 March, pp. 2, 26; translation). Gerry Gosselin's text in *Le Devoir* was written as an open letter to Campbell:

> We believe, Mr. President, that in the name of order and discipline you have done a disservice to a sense of justice ... You have been hiding for too long behind words that you do not know the meaning of: authority, justice, order, discipline. These ideologies are poorly serviced by the personal rancour that motivates your decisions (18 March, p. 13; translation).

So it seems that for French Canadians, the punishment was obviously disproportionate and could be explained by the desire of Campbell, who had become the symbol of the English oppressor, to curb the success of one of their own.

The Riot: Political Mobilization and Affirmation of the "Little People"

The collective anger of French Canadians seemed to have reached a climax on the evening of 17 March when the Canadiens faced the Detroit Red Wings. Various photos and eyewitness accounts published in the newspapers on 18 and 19 March 1955 suggest that a "rupture" had occurred in the dominant/dominated social order. Everything suggested that "the little submissive people" had mobilized to demonstrate their rebellion against what they saw as an injustice and as discrimination towards one of their own. There was a record crowd at the Forum (16,000 spectators); an equally imposing crowd of demonstrators (estimated at 10,000) had gathered outside the building, brandishing eloquent placards: "Campbell Out," "Long Live Richard," "Unfair to French Canadians," "Richard persecuted," and so on. If we believe the account of a police officer present during the demonstrations, these were in fact the common people, not hooligans: "What really struck me was seeing a pregnant woman there. She was there, in the crowd. We had to push her. I asked myself, what is she doing here? I was really shocked by the people I saw there."[13] It was as if, through a profound emotional identification with Richard, the "little people" had decided to no longer submit. They were going to fight if they had to, like Richard on the ice.

Campbell's arrival at the arena set off the "rebellion." According to the testimony collected by Cyr and Leblanc, a group of fans from the "little people" (Édouard Latreille, a garage mechanic, his friends Marcel Desmarais, Denis Gendron, and André Parent, and a few others) had brought various projectiles, including a tear gas canister, intending to throw them at the "English authorities." When Campbell took his usual seat, objects started to fly towards him, then the tear gas canister exploded, causing spectators to rush out in confusion. Meanwhile, what was called a riot was happening outside the Forum: tramcars were overturned, fires were lit in various places, all kinds of objects were thrown at the Forum, and there were acts of vandalism and looting along St Catherine Street; damage was estimated at around $100,000. No deaths or injuries were reported; it was "quiet" rebellion.

Did the Richard/Campbell affair "change" French Canadians? When questioned by Cyr and Leblanc, Claude Larochelle, a sports reporter at the time, thought it had: "What surprised me is that something is happening in that little people that was parading on Saint-Jean-Baptiste Day with its poor little shorn sheep, with exceptional discipline, who were packing the churches every Sunday and who obeyed all the laws and all the rules of the police" (translation).

Sporting events, especially hockey games, are often occasions for disturbances and violence. I could mention, for example, the rampage following the Canadiens victory in the 1986 Stanley Cup final and, more recently, the riot in Vancouver after the Canucks lost the 2011 Stanley Cup final to the Boston Bruins.[14] But, the demonstration of 17 March 1955 stood out from both of these, for it would have social and political significance and impact. The different perceptions and analyses of the event between the anglophone and francophone press of the time attest to this. If it had been solely about the sporting event, how to explain the contrasting coverage in terms of the English and French newspapers? The vast majority of articles and editorials in the anglophone press praised Campbell for his courage in the face of public protest and expressed indignation over the behaviour of the "hooligans"; the francophone press accused him of *causing* those disturbances. The excerpts below provide an overview of this antagonism and probably reflect the opinions prevalent in the two ethnic groups in Montreal.

The day after the riot, on 18 March, the *Montreal Star* ran this banner headline on the front page: "President of NHL Is Victim of Attack." Baz O'Meara began his sports editorial as follows:

> You have to admire courage, no matter where you find it. President Clarence Campbell of the NHL showed it last night in an almost foolhardy

> fashion. He was the storm centre of incidents disgraceful in the extreme, but which were powered inside the Forum by a group of young hotheads bent on destruction, mayhem and possibly arson. You can question his judgement in facing that jeering crowd, in virtually taking a chance on physical injury, but you can't fault his fortitude. (18 March, p. 4).

The *Globe and Mail* also remarked on Campbell's courage and denounced those who dared to blame him:

> Mr. Clarence Campbell did his duty by Canadian sport in general, and Canadian hockey in particular. He was late in doing it but he did it. The result was a shocking exhibition of mob violence and hysteria in and around the Montreal Forum Thursday night. No less shocking, indeed more so, are the attempts of Montreal civic officials to blame Mr. Campbell for provoking that violence ... Mr. Campbell showed a great deal of firmness in suspending Richard, and a great deal of courage in attending Thursday night's game. (19 March, p. 6)

The other dominant theme in the anglophone press was condemnation of the "hooligans" responsible for the shame that was now a stain on Montreal. Under the headline "A Black Eye for Montreal," the editorialist for the *Montreal Star* wrote:

> A mob's explosion explodes the mob itself. But what can we say to explain in decent terms to ourselves the hangover of humiliation that remains ... Montreal today stands convicted of emotional instability and lack of discipline. It can take no pride in what has happened. Nothing but shame remains. (18 March, p. 10)

Dink Carroll of *The Gazette* attributed the riot essentially to young hooligans, refusing to acknowledge that the events had any political significance. Note that the archival photos and films do not agree with his description:

> The disgraceful scenes were sparked by a small group of youths, either in their teens or just out of them. They wore black leather windbreakers, almost like a uniform, with white lettering on the back. They form themselves into Jolly Roger clubs and travel around on motor bikes. (19 March, p. 8)

The francophone press analysed the events in a diametrically opposite way. For example, under the headline "Campbell n'a eu de considération que pour lui," ("Campbell thought only of himself"), Armand Jokisch of *Dimanche-Matin* declared:

> The English-language newspapers have made a big deal about the backbone and courage shown by Clarence Sutherland Campbell by coming to the Forum for the match last Thursday evening. We regret to say that we cannot agree. In our view Mr. Campbell is nothing but a windbag and a demagogue who is not afraid to risk the lives of hundreds of people to satisfy his personal pride. Campbell alone is responsible for this whole affair, even putting aside his verdict in the Richard case. He issued a clear challenge to the population and it took up the challenge as it should have. (20 March, p. 28; translation)

The front page of the *Montréal-Matin* of 18 March ran the headline: "Émeute, rue Ste-Catherine. Campbell chassé du Forum" (Riot, St. Catherine Street, Campbell chased from the Forum) and "Campbell a provoqué Montréal" ("Campbell provoked Montreal"). In his comments, the editorialist excused the crowd and accused Campbell:

> And it is this same [Montreal] public that Campbell has penalized and challenged through his language, his declarations and his performance on television. The public, which has been scorned, the public that has watched the battles, has lost its temper. *It did as Richard did, it hit back* ... Those responsible are Campbell and the governors of the National Hockey League. (19 March, p. 4; my emphasis; translation)

Under the headline "Démission de Campbell réclamée. Sa présence au Forum cause une émeute sans précédent" ("Campbell's resignation called For. His presence at the Forum caused an unprecedented riot"), Phil Séguin, sports columnist at *La Patrie*, wrote:

> Campbell, who was appointed to his position at the instigation of Conn Smythe, a well-known "mange-canadien", made his most recent and his most serious blunder when he dared to confront more than 15,000 people and virtually laughed in their faces after having, with an unfair, arbitrary decision, based on contradictory, muddled testimony, suspended the greatest star of modern hockey, Maurice Richard, for the rest of the regular season and the playoffs ... Everyone who watched those 20 minutes of hockey last night will remember for a long time that it was Campbell who caused, by his stubborn presence at the Forum, the riot that caused approximately

> $100,000 in damage to the Forum and elsewhere on St. Catherine Street. (18 March, p. 27; translation)

The front page of *La Presse* expressed similar views under the headline: "Défi et provocation de Campbell. Le président n'aurait pas dû aller au Forum" ("Challenge and provocation by Campbell. The president should not have gone to the Forum"). The article read:

> The chief magistrate of the metropolis has expressed the opinion that, as inexcusable as it is, the disturbance was provoked by the presence of Mr. Campbell at the Forum. Campbell, said the mayor, should have acted more sensibly by refraining from attending the Canadians–Detroit match, or at least not announce ahead of time his visit as he did. His presence, in fact, could be interpreted as a veritable challenge. (18 March 1955, p. 1; translation)

Finally, we must mention the joke, written in capital letters, by Gerry Gosselin in *Le Devoir*, after Richard had publicly issued a call for calm: "Maurice Richard has to come to the rescue of Clarence Campbell to get him out of a dead-end. The vanquished, once again, comes to the rescue of the conqueror" (19 March 1955, p. 13; translation).

The Richard/Campbell Affair: A Collective Awakening

The riot at the Montreal Forum was even reported in American and European newspapers – a visibility that in retrospect might seem excessive, given that the incidents were in fact much less serious than those that have occurred more recently – in Vancouver, for example. But it was mostly in Quebec and in Canadian society that the impact was felt profoundly. Reflections on and analyses of the event fuelled discussions long after the riot, both in the newspapers and among the population. André Laurendeau's column in *Le Devoir* of 21 March titled "On a tué mon frère Richard" ("They killed my brother Richard") proposed to French Canadians a reading of the events that perhaps helped further strengthen the French Canadian awakening that had been spurred by the Richard/Campbell affair. Some key excerpts:

> French-Canadian nationalism appears to have taken refuge in hockey. The crowd that shouted its anger last Thursday evening was not motivated only by enthusiasm for sport or feelings of an injustice committed against

> its idol. It was a frustrated people that was protesting against its fate. Destiny, on Thursday night, was called Campbell, but he embodies all the real or imaginary enemies that this people encounters ... For this little people, in French Canada, Maurice Richard is a kind of revenge (we take them where you can). He is really one of a kind, and he was going to prove it again this year ... However, along comes Campbell to kill his momentum. They are depriving French Canadians of the Maurice Richard who was going to establish more clearly his superiority. And this "they" speaks English, this "they" decides in haste against the hero, provoke, arouse. So he will see. People are suddenly tired of having always had masters, of having for a long time submitted. Mr. Campbell will see. [This] brief outburst reveals what has been dormant behind the apparent indifference and the long passivity of French Canadians. (21 March, p. 2; translation).

This strongly ideological editorial might suggest that the political meaning of the riot was "owned" by the French Canadian intelligentsia. Actually, the testimonies of people who demonstrated that night, as collected by Cyr and Leblanc, suggest that it was a grassroots movement that was not going to fade quickly. Some examples:

> He showed us, in a game, what we wanted to have in our lives: go toward a goal the way he went toward the goal, to score. We wanted that in the way we lived, but we still didn't have someone to whip us up. Anyway, he gave us an example. (Marcel Desmarais, demonstrator)
>
> Maurice Richard really represented us in every respect, without maybe knowing it himself. His spirit, his energy and his will to succeed went beyond all the norms. While the rest of us were caught up in it, he himself was coming out, coming out of prison, you could say, with his skates, his desire to overcome. He really represented the people. (Donald Lafleur, demonstrator)
>
> People realized then that they could stand up, that there might be consequences, but that you won't go to hell because of it. (Claude Larochelle, sports reporter) (translation)

It seems that the affair's political impact did not escape the attention of anglophones either. Katz indicated this in his in-depth article in *Maclean's* on 17 September:

> Frank D. Corbett, a citizen of Westmount, expressed an opinion about the riot which many people thought about but few discussed publicly.

> In a letter to the editor of a local paper, he said bluntly that the outbreak was symptomatic of racial ill-feeling. "French and English relationships have deteriorated badly over the past 10 years and they have never been worse," he wrote.
>
> "The basic unrest is nationalism, which is ever present in Quebec. Let's face it ... The French Canadians want the English expelled from the province." (17 September, p. 14)

Finally, although it is in hindsight, the testimony of Phyllis King Campbell collected by Cyr and Leblanc seems significant to us:

> "I remember that one time [Clarence Campbell] said that it had been the beginning of the Quiet Revolution."
> "Is that what he thought?"
> "I think so. He thought it had something to do with what followed."

The Political Effectiveness of the Sports World

In conclusion, it can be said that after the riot, Maurice Richard became part of the mythology of the French Canadian people: the power relationships between dominant and dominated that he embodied would survive him. So we can understand how he was able to contribute to the Quiet Revolution while being publicly "apolitical" as he continued his career.

The political elite and the intelligentsia are inclined to think that the sports world plays a secondary role in social debates, because sports are play. We believe, on the contrary, that the lack of understanding of its active role in the collective imaginary gives sport a political effectiveness that is all the greater. It is too often forgotten that sports feature social actors who quickly become symbols and that they affect people's sense of identity as well as their affective dimension. It follows that its effectiveness in mobilizing and activating communities is sometimes greater than any number of ideological speeches. The Richard/Campbell affair constitutes, in our view, an eloquent illustration of this, since it led to a *popular* uprising and acted as a catalyst for the affirmation of Quebecers.

NOTES

1 An earlier version of this article was published in 2003 in *Bulletin d'histoire politique*, 11(2), pp. 30–44.

2 According to *Canadian Advertising* (1955, 28 [2], 25–51), the circulation of the newspapers chosen was as follows: *La Presse*, 230,380; *Le Montréal-Matin*, 65,363; *Le Devoir*, 24,180; *La Patrie*, 15,383; *Globe and Mail*, 244,391; *Montreal Star*, 154,902; *The Herald*, 38,873.

3 Note that the nationalism of Maurice Duplessis was more rhetorical than authentic and had little in common with Richard's nationalist sentiments. Richard's defence of the "little people" was, in fact, incompatible with the reign of terror and the suppression of civil liberties that characterized the Duplessis regime.

4 Richard was the first francophone hockey player to have a newspaper column, which only increased the admiration that ordinary people had for him.

5 *Samedi-Dimanche*, 28 June 1952, p. 43; 2 August 1952, p. 30; translation. The second excerpt followed up a previous article in which Richard approved the fact that Bernard Geoffrion had had the opportunity to learn English; Richard was afraid that what he said would be interpreted as distancing himself from his francophone allegiance.

6 During that period, the term "Canayens" designated French Canadians; "English" meant English Canadians.

7 Quoted in Pellerin (1998, pp. 241–242); translation. My emphasis. Note that this text by Richard was quoted and condemned by many commentators in the anglophone press, in particular by Gord Walker in his column in the *Globe and Mail* of 17 March 1955. For many French Canadians, these criticisms made Richard's boldness and courage even more admirable.

8 Quebec slang for a "fearful person," from the pejorative term "Pea Souper" that anglophones gave to francophones. The popular belief was that pea soup was an everyday food for francophones.

9 Quoted by Pellerin (1998, p. 260); translation. My emphasis.

10 Other criticisms are mentioned by Gord Walker, *The Globe and Mail*, Toronto, 9 January 1954.

11 Although all Campbell's communications were in English, this fact provided the opportunity for the Montréal-Matin editor to denounced this usual lack of respect: "Before concluding on this overly long statement of Campbell, full of mistakes, we will take the liberty of reminding the president that the French language is official in the country. When being so severe with respect to the idol of the French Canadians, it seems that Campbell could have at least had the decency to provide French-language journalists with press releases written in their language. While translating his excessively long and insipid article, we felt ourselves getting more and more irritated" (17 March, p. 25; translation).

12 A few English journalists nevertheless refused to go along with this tendency by denouncing Campbell and supporting Richard, in particular Jack Kinsella in the *Ottawa Citizen* and Andy O'Brien in the *Standard* and the *Montreal Star*.
13 Words of Jacques Laurin, police officer (translation). This perception contrasts with that of Phyllis King, secretary and later wife of Clarence Campbell, who stated: "In the street, there were the usual fans. There were a lot of hooligans who were there to have a good time. All that because of a player who got punished!" Comments reported by Cyr and Leblanc, 1999.
14 For an analysis of mob violence at sporting events, including the 1955 riot, see the doctoral thesis by Michel Marois (1993), as well as Duperreault, 1981.

2 The Passion of the Canadiens on the Red Line: Between Faith and Idolatry[1]

OLIVIER BAUER

"All the *loyal fans* of the *Sainte-Flanelle*, those who listen *religiously* to the hockey games of the Canadiens, hoped for a *miraculous* season, but it turned into a *calvary*, a *way of the cross*, a *descent into hell*. The *idols* played without *soul* and even though those who had their *baptism* in the National Hockey League struggle *body and soul* to remain *in the good graces* of the *Great Manitou*, they were sometimes *sacrificed* when they were forced to leave for other *heavens*. Jacques Martin's job was *Herculean*. *Jesus Price* was *crucified*, *Brother André* was sent to *purgatory* and even Plekanec was *nailed* to the bench. Fortunately, Halak was a *saviour*, Cammalleri finally *exorcised his demons*, by *coming back from the dead* to *preach* by example and play like a *god*. But there were no *miracle* solutions – goals do not fall from *heaven!* – and the coup de *grace* was losing against these *damned Devils*. This setback was almost *a death knell* for the hopes of *Glorieux*. Let's hope that the break is *salutary*, that next year, we will be able to *praise* the players, that they will finally bring home the *Saint-Graal, the silver chalice to the Mecca of hockey and that they will appear in the Temple of Hockey, in the pantheon of ice sports for eternity. Inch'Halak!*"

The Canadiens: A Religion in Quebec

This text, made up almost completely of expressions found in the media – radio, television, newspapers, Internet sites – demonstrates, if proof was needed, that in Montreal and throughout Quebec, the Canadiens are not only a hockey club, not only an entertainment business, not only a cultural phenomenon, not only a social fact. For some people, in certain circumstances, it seems to fulfil the functions of a religion. But is it really? We need to carefully check the phenomenon against a definition of religion to see if the Canadiens meet the criteria. Religion is:

> human beings' relation to that which they regard as holy, sacred, spiritual, or divine. Religion is commonly regarded as consisting of a person's relation to God or to gods or spirits. Worship is probably the most basic element of religion, but moral conduct, right belief, and participation in *religious institutions are generally also constituent elements of the religious life as practiced by believers and* worshipers and as commanded by religious sages and scriptures.[2]

The essential element of a religion seems to me to be this "personal relationship with God, with gods or with spirits." In the introduction to a collection I co-edited on the theme of the religion of the Canadiens, I concluded, a little too quickly, that what was lacking with the Canadiens team was "a presumed and explicit reference to something ultimately transcendent – to a Divinity, whatever S/He may be" (Bauer and Barreau, 2009, p. 29; translation). I should have known that on questions of religion nothing is ever definitive. In fact, there are gods in hockey, and the religion of the Habs is a way to relate to them.

The Gods of Hockey

When francophone Quebecers comment on a hockey game, they all have the same curious habit of giving life to the puck. The puck hops, jumps, and deflects on its own. In the end, the puck can roll in favour of either team.

While I do not want to put too much emphasis on this kind of expression – it could just be a cliché or a verbal tic – I would like to take it seriously and consider that, at least for sports journalists, the puck has "her" own life (in French, "puck" is a feminine noun). There are times when "she" is no longer under the players' control, when "she" is freed from the physical laws of gravity and friction. For example, when the puck deflects over the glass, it is always by accident. But what does that really mean? I can see only two possible answers: either the puck is acting independently, or it is being manipulated by some superior power, by destiny, or by the gods of hockey. And in Montreal, these gods have a name. They are called the Ghosts of the Forum, the ghosts who were Howie Morenz, Maurice Richard, Patrick Roy, and the fourteen other players who permitted the Canadiens to win their twenty-four Stanley

Cups – all on their old rink in the Forum – and whose jerseys have been retired.

Think of what that implies! If the puck is animate, if it moves under the control of a superior being, then playing hockey must require more than talent, more than tough training and healthy living (which is, in a way, the "moral conduct" required by every religion), more than a wealthy franchise (which is the "religious institution"), and more than a generous owner, a sensible general manager, and a competent coach (three kinds of "religious sages"). All of those human attributes must be required. But they will not be enough!

And as proof, it is enough to remember that the same team, with the same players and the same coach, with the same equipment and in the same rink, can easily win one day and lose miserably the next. The glorious uncertainty of sport! If hockey gods exist, winning requires that the fans believe in their team whatever happens – their "belief" – and that they watch the games – their "worship." But this alone does not make the Canadiens a religion. To win matches and trophies, the players, the coach, the leaders, and the fans must maintain this "personal relationship with God, gods or spirits," and they must celebrate a superior being, which could be the puck itself (just think of the players or fans who carefully keep the puck of their first goal or of an important match), the Ghosts of the Forum, or the God of any more traditional religion.

If the puck is considered to be alive or under the control of some more or less well-defined superior being, it is easy to understand the behaviour of players, coaches, leaders, and fans, their superstitions, their rituals, their prayers, even their obsessions. They try to control the puck, to make it "roll the right way" – which is necessarily always the way they and their team want it to roll. They try to limit the unexpected, the unpredictable. They try to ward off evil spells and gain the favour of the superior being, *mysterium fascinans et tremendum*, fascinating and terrifying, like everything that is sacred. As in all rituals, they want to give a little in order to receive much more, according to the principle of *do ut des* or the gift and countergift (Van der Leeuw, 1938; Mauss, 1966).

State of Grace

As Jesus was transfigured, as mystics can attain ecstasy and epektasis, as Buddhists can reach Nirvana, as Hindus can merge with Shiva, players can be "in the zone," "catch a *bounce*," and experience moments when everything works for them and nothing seems impossible.

Patrick Roy (Saint Patrick in the religion of the Canadiens) experienced countless remarkable moments. But there was one that was really exceptional. On 11 April 1986, the goaltender was barely twenty years old, playing his first season with the Habs. He was playing against the Rangers in Madison Square Garden in New York City, in the third game of the conference final. The game was tied 1–1 at the end of regulation time. During overtime, the young goalie stopped everything fired at him and the Canadiens won the game 2–1. Roy will remember that game his whole life. Twenty-two years later, when the Canadiens were retiring his jersey, he said in an interview: "To be honest with you, the overtime was the best feeling I ever had. It happened a couple of times ... But that night somehow I could do whatever I wanted. I think I could have left my net and the guys would have still shot it at me. I'm joking, but I felt so good. I knew that nothing could get past me."[3]

But grace touches not only the Habs' goaltenders. Sometimes it also helps out other players. On 16 January 2006, the Washington Capitals were playing the Phoenix Coyotes. Alexander Ovechkin, Alexander the Great in NHL mythology, was twenty-one years old. This is important, because grace seems to love the innocence of youth. The Russian player got the puck at centre ice. He went to the right side, then tried to return to the centre, going around a Coyotes defenceman. But his opponent resisted. Ovechkin skated past the net and fell down. He was on this back, his head away from the net. But he kept control of the puck. Blindly, with the end of his stick, he was able to push the puck behind his back and score a goal that no human being could have scored without the help of the hockey gods. They should have been credited with an assist.

Patrick Roy and Alexander Ovechkin! It was almost bound to happen that I would mention a goalie and a top scorer. Not because they receive more grace than a defenceman or a referee, who also have their moments of grace, but because they make grace more visible, more obvious. Patrick Roy and Alexander Ovechkin. Talking about a goalie and a goal scorer also reminds us that in hockey, as in any sport, paradise for one player is hell for another.

"Dipped Them in Holy Water"

When they comment on a lucky victory by the Canadiens, Quebecers sometimes use this rather crude expression. They say that the players "have dipped them in holy water." The pronoun "them" does not refer here to the hands of the players, or to their feet, but to a more private part of their anatomy.

The expression is very significant. It says a lot about the devotion Quebecers have for the Canadiens, since it refers to a typically Catholic devotion: dipping one's fingers in the holy water before entering the church, for the purpose of sanctification and purification. Of course, applied to the Canadiens, it is just a metaphor. No one would dare imagine the players really doing what the expression suggests ...

But the expression reveals a very religious, very Christian, and very Catholic way of thinking: there are wins for which the players do not deserve all the credit; you can ask for God's help by performing certain rituals; therefore, when the Canadiens win an undeserved victory, it was with God's help; and to obtain God's help, the Canadiens have to perform the required rituals.

The expression defines the Habs' religion as Catholicism. It catholicizes the God from whom the fans of the Canadiens are expecting help, because he is the only God who will respond to such rituals. Of course, the fact that the religion of the Canadiens is marked by Catholicism is no surprise in a Quebec that was massively Catholic and still largely is, at least culturally.

Believing Against All Evidence to the Contrary

I will add one last indicator to show that the Canadiens are a religion. There was a time – from the 1950s to the 1970s – when the superiority of the Canadiens was not an act of faith but a well-established fact. Any reasonable person had to acknowledge that the Stanley Cup belonged in Montreal, where it came back almost every year. But times have changed! And since 1993, the Canadiens have failed, year after year, to bring home the cup. Currently, no reasonable person would seriously declare that the Canadiens are the best team in the NHL. Certainly no one would state it as a fact. You could say it as a profession of personal conviction.

The religion of the Canadiens requires having confidence in the Canadiens no matter what happens, hoping, year after year, that the cup will come back to Montreal. During the famine years, the Canadiens compel their loyal fans to believe, against all odds, and despite the weaknesses of the team, their injuries, the lack of francophone players, problems hiring top players, despite all the problems experienced by the players – on the ice and in the city – by the managers, and by the owners, not to mention pressure from the media. The fans have no choice but to be loyal and believe!

Reacting to the idea that the Canadiens are a religion, a mischievous blogger wrote about the Toronto Maple Leafs: "Cheering for the Leafs is like going to church when you know there's no God."[4] He was wrong, of course. Because a true believer supports his team whatever happens, precisely because he believes there is a God and believes He can help the team.

Making the Canadiens into a Religion

Until now, a religion of the Habs has remained theoretical, impersonal. But in Montreal, it is not hard to find examples of people who really do mix the hockey club with religion. In my research, I have identified two ways of doing this, which I will label with the first names of people who, spontaneously, have wanted to share them with me. There will therefore be Victoria's way and Théodore's way. They are quite different.

Victoria uses her Catholic faith to make sure the Habs win. Therefore, her way belongs to an inclusive model, one in which sports is included in religion. Théodore, on the other hand, has made the Canadiens his own religion. Théodore's way belongs to a syncretic model, in which sport and religion are blended (Bauer, 2009).

Victoria's Way

In 2009, after taking part in a broadcast on Radio Ville-Marie, a Catholic station in Montreal, I received an e-mail from a listener. Here is what she wrote:

> My daughter Victoria ... had given [a] school presentation on Brother André ... She distributed medals and statuettes of Brother André to each of her classmates (surprisingly everyone was very happy with the gifts). The same evening, the whole family was at the Bell Centre, invited to a box seat to watch the match between the Canadiens and the Rangers on 19 February 2008 ... The Habs were crushed, I remember, maybe 5–0. I suggested that my daughter (then 11 years old) ask Brother André for help. He owed her given the "apostolic publicity" she had given him that very day in her class! No sooner said than done, and with each prayer, bam ... a goal for the Canadiens. And it went on and on. The other guests couldn't believe their eyes.

> I had to confess to them that Victoria was imploring Brother André for help (she's the kind of person who quickly gets favours from Heaven, but she doesn't overdo it, unfortunately!). In the end, the whole gang in the box seat congratulated Brother André. I really had the impression that the Blessed was playing with the team. The Rangers admitted in the press that they didn't understand: "The puck flew on its own straight into the net." We really saw it as supernatural intervention, which I can say without being sanctimonious. In the elevator, Victoria, saw the happy people and she told me, "You know, it's thanks to me that they're happy and they don't know it ... Well, also thanks to Brother André." The next day, the media reported on the match of the century, incomparable and never equalled ... That only increased Victoria's feelings of pride and, at the same time, her confidence in Brother André. Except that she has kept that secret the fact that she got Brother André to play with the Canadiens on that remarkable February 19, 2008. (translation)

Victoria is not an isolated case in Montreal. She is not alone in thinking that the saints of the Catholic tradition can help the Canadiens. In fact, the devotion of Canadiens fans is closely associated with those saints – with two in particular, Saint Joseph and Saint Brother André, and with the oratory founded by the latter and dedicated to the former. Pilgrims go to the oratory to gain favours from the two saints, favours they obtain, for example, by climbing on their knees the stairs leading to it, by lighting candles in front of portraits of Saint Joseph or by touching Brother André's casket. When Canadiens fans have doubts, when they no longer believe the Canadiens can win on their own, they do not hesitate to climb the mountain to plead for help from Saint Joseph and Brother André.

On 14 April 2010, one day before the Habs began the first round of playoffs against the Washington Capitals, the CKAC-Sports radio station organized a pilgrimage to the oratory. Informed by a student, I decided to attend. There were approximately twenty young adults, wearing Canadiens jerseys – two "Maurice Richards" and two "Jean Béliveaus," of course, and a "Carey Price," already classic, but also a "Scott Gomez," which was more unexpected. Gathering on the terrace, they conducted a brief parody of a mass dedicated to the Canadiens, with the radio host acting as officiant. Then they went down into the crypt to light candles to ask for help from Saint Joseph.

Of course, they were doing it primarily for the media. But once the journalists were gone, several participants discreetly lit their own candles. "I did it to ask that no one get injured during the playoffs," one of them confided in me.

Théodore's Way

Théodore's way is quite different. Instead of using his Christian faith, or any other tradition, to help the Canadiens, Théodore – seriously or not, it is impossible to know – has made the Habs the object of his religion.

Théodore is a university student. He has a Facebook page titled "Temple du Hockey (des Canadiens)." It shows twenty-seven pictures of the temple of the Canadiens that he has built in his own apartment. The temple consists of a room full of relics and liturgical objects, all to the glory of the Habs. There are Canadiens jerseys, Canadiens flags, Canadiens pucks, Canadiens sticks, figurines of Canadiens players, and so on. There is even a seat from the old Forum, which Théodore only sits in during Habs playoff games.

In the centre of the room, Théodore has built an altar, with four steps, one for each round in the playoffs, built using twenty pucks with the Canadiens logo. In front, he has placed figurines of Canadiens players, which he has flanked with two candles, one red and the other white. On the highest step, Théodore has placed a small replica of the Stanley Cup.

Does Théodore really have faith in the Canadiens? Only he can answer that. But neither on his Facebook page, nor in any of the conversations I have had with him, has Théodore ever given any indication that all of this might be just a huge joke.

In any case, the photographs show clearly a kind of piety directed at the Canadiens. When it comes to them, Théodore does not have faith in a god, but he does believe in some superior being whom he thinks is able and willing to help them. In Théodore's religion, the Canadiens occupy the place of God, of the divine, of the absolute, of the sacred, of the Force – I do not know what name Théodore would give to it.

But it should be pointed out that Théodore organizes his Canadiens religion from a very Catholic perspective, which, once again, is hardly surprising in Quebec. His temple reproduces precisely the model of a Catholic church, with its centre aisle, its side chapel, its relics, its altar, and its liturgical vases. The differences are minimal but significant. The Stanley Cup has replaced the chalice or the monstrance. And on the wall, where we would expect to find a crucifix, there is a Habs jersey.

The Dogmas of the Canadiens Religion

I think I have erased any doubts about the existence of a Canadiens religion. This is not just a theologian trying to impose a religious dimension on a cultural phenomenon: it is clearly shown in the two cases of Victoria and Théodore, however different they are. Like all religions, it has dogmas according to which the faithful are supposed to lead their lives. Some are specific to it, others come from elsewhere. I would like to highlight three of them.

One Dogma of Hockey: "You Will Be a Man!"

As explained by Canadian theologian Tom Sinclair-Faulkner, hockey promotes three main values: "In the hockey cosmos one is Canadian, one is manly (a quality which goes beyond sheer masculinity), and that one is excellent (by which I mean something that has more to do with winning than with the ancient Greek notion of *arete*)" (2005, p. 391). I will now examine the first value, but expressed in a different way: "In the world of the Canadiens, one is a Quebecer." And I will set aside the third, which seems to me too broad to be specific to the Canadiens or even to hockey. But the second one, virility or masculinity, seems to me to be very important for all men's hockey teams, including for the Canadiens. I therefore make it the first dogma of the Canadiens religion.

It is always strange – and a little disturbing – when a man feels he needs to prove he is a man. Being a man should not require proof. Being a man should be simply a matter of fact. What could give rise to the need to prove it, if not the fear of not being one or not being seen as one? But after all, perhaps such a fear is not illegitimate in a sport in which the players are always wearing a cup and garters! In hockey, you have to be manly, and this manliness corresponds to very precise stereotypes. I will give two examples: the "playoff beard," and the goalie's face.

The playoff beard is a good way to show on your face how successful your team is. It first appeared with the New York Islanders in the early 1980s, and the logic is simple: the longer the beard, the longer the team has played in the playoffs and therefore the better it is. The playoff beard is also a good way to show your virility, because it makes it possible to distinguish the men from the boys, which is the role attributed to it in the playoffs. The playoff beard therefore fulfils the function of an institutional ritual as defined by Pierre Bourdieu; that is, it is an attempt to transform cultural differences into natural ones, to acknowledge that the adult is the one who has the beard, which is one way to define adulthood. But there is still more behind the playoff beard. Bourdieu showed that the first function of institutional rituals, such as circumcision, was the least obvious, the most secret. "The act of institution is an act of social magic that can create difference *ex nihilo,* or else (as is more often the case) by exploiting as it were pre-existing differences, like the biological differences between the sexes" (1991, pp. 119–120; translation).

From this perspective, the true meaning of the playoff beard becomes obvious. Its role is not to indicate which players took part in the playoffs, nor is it to distinguish adult players from child players. The playoff beard exists primarily to establish a difference between those who can, who could, and who will be able to grow a beard – that is, all men, whatever their talent as hockey players – and those who cannot, and could not, and will not be able to – that is, all women, whatever their talent as hockey players. It therefore becomes obvious that the true function of the playoff beard is to make hockey manly by excluding women.

There is another domain, much less symbolic, in which hockey constructs its concept of virility, defined by physical courage. Hockey demands that players be ready to offer their own bodies for the good of the team. And in the history of hockey, the greatest sacrifices were made by the goalies. They gave so much of themselves to meet the expectations placed on them, to fulfil what was considered their duty, especially during the long period when they played barefaced. In an absolutely fascinating book, Jim Hynes and Gary Smith (2008) recall the long history of goaltenders' sufferings, from 1 January 1918, when the National Hockey League gave goalkeepers permission to dive to the ice, and 7 April 1974, when Andy Brown was the last goalie who "defended his team's net bare-faced" (2008, p. 94), plus the day Jacques Plante set a scandalous precedent by being the first NHL goalie to wear a protective mask. That was on 1 November 1959 in Madison Square Garden in New York City. What seems so self-evident today took a long time to be accepted. While winning the right to protect his face, the Canadiens goalie faced many problems and a great deal of resistance. "I had to show good results to keep the mask," Plante would say later. But even though he did, he still had to put up with teammates, reporters, and fans who suggested he was a coward (2008, p. 50).

Of course, the confusion between masculinity and stupidity, between experience and scars, between courage and recklessness, does not concern only goaltenders. It was not until 1979 that the NHL made helmets mandatory, and it was only in 2013 that the NHL made visors standard for all new players in the league. Fortunately, the players themselves are redefining masculinity in hockey. A survey conducted in 2007 by the *Globe and Mail* found that nearly half the players in the National Hockey League wore a visor or face shield. Times have changed since 2004, when commentator Don Cherry could say – in an accurate statement, but obviously not very politically correct – that "only French Canadian players and Europeans wear visors."

The world of hockey took a long time to admit that masculinity was not measured by the number of scars a player had on his face. It should be noted that the French Canadian and European players were a little quicker to understand this, since they were the first to reinterpret the dogma of virility.

A Dogma in Quebec: "You'll Speak French!"

> We were 10, 11 or 12 years old. It was a little like [the film] *The Dog Who Stopped the War*. It was in a working-class neighbourhood of Montreal. Kids faced off, three against three, street against street, anglos against francos. They dressed in the blue of the *Leafs*, the enemy, us in the red of the Canadiens. Blue, white, red: the most beautiful jersey in the history of the sport. (Trudel, 2001, p. 12; translation)

If the Canadiens are a religion in Quebec, then in the memories of Pierre Trudel they should resemble the world of *The Hockey Sweater* by Roch Carrier, a world in which the children spend their winter between three places, "the school, the church and the skating rink," in which, if you recited a prayer, it was to "ask God to help us play as well as Maurice Richard," in which the young priest was the referee, in which the player who misbehaved had to "go to the church and ask God to forgive [him]," in which a little Quebecer could not wear the sweater of the Toronto Maple Leafs, because they were anglophones and, no doubt, because they were Protestants, in which the victim could ask God "to send me right away, a hundred millions moths to eat up my Toronto Maple Leafs sweater" (Carrier, 1984).

In Quebec's collective memory or collective unconsciousness, the Canadiens player must be a Quebecer and therefore speak French and be Catholic. But the facts contradict this representation, transforming it into a dogma to be believed rather than an observation to be made. I will present three arguments that invalidate the dogma of a francophone essence of the Canadiens.

First of all, in 1909, the Club Athlétique Canadien (the original name of the Canadiens) was founded by two anglophone businessmen, Jimmy Gardner, one of the owners of the Wanderers, a well-established anglophone hockey club in Montreal, and John Ambrose O'Brien, the owner of the Renfrew Millionaires, an Ontario hockey team. They founded this new team to increase the number of games played in Montreal, to create more rivalry and more interest in hockey, and to reach a new clientele among Montreal's francophones. Their goal was so obvious that a journalist with *Le Devoir*, Tancrède Marsil, accused O'Brien of trying to "harvest in the East [of Montreal] some good dough" (Bonneau and Hafsi, 1996, p. 35; translation). In that time, despite its nickname, the Canadiens were not the team *of* the "Canadiens," a term that then designated the francophones of Canada.

Second, the Canadiens were never an entirely francophone team. For its first official game (a 7–3 victory against the Silver Kings of Cobalt, Ontario, on 5 January 1910), it already had an anglophone player, Newsy Lalonde (notwithstanding his French name), who came from Cornwall, Ontario (Guay, 1990, p. 259). The team has never made hiring francophones a priority. It has always tried to recruit the best players, whatever their language. Howie Morenz, for example, the first great star of the Canadiens, was born in Mitchell, Ontario. His parents were immigrants from Switzerland. He was Protestant, and it was the "Very Reverend Malcolm Campbell, Moderator of the General Assembly of the Presbyterian Church of Canada" (Goyens, Turowetz, and Dugay, 1996, p. 38) who presided over his funeral in the Forum, on 10 March 1937, in front of 50,000 people.

Finally, the colour of the Canadiens' sweater reveals the full ambiguity of its identity. In sports, the colour worn is rarely inconsequential. In English soccer, for example, when a city has two high-level teams and distinction is made on a confessional basis, red is the colour of the Catholic team, such as Manchester United or Liverpool, and blue the colour of the Protestant team, Manchester City or Everton. We could apply that model in Canada and say that the Canadiens wear a red jersey because they come from a Catholic province and that the Leafs wear a blue jersey because they come from a Protestant city. But in Canada, the symbolism of colours follows different rules. Blue is the colour of Quebec, red the colour of Canada. Should we therefore conclude that the colour of their jerseys makes the Canadiens more a Canadian team than a Quebec team? I believe we can, especially if we compare them to the Quebec Nordiques, who during their brief existence wore a jersey that very obviously reproduced the Quebec flag: blue with white fleurs-de-lis. And it is perhaps because the red makes the team too Canadian that no one has ever nicknamed the Canadiens "the red" – as the athletes of McGill University are called Red Men. Rather, they are "le Tricolore," which makes sense, given that the Canadiens colours are red, white, and blue. That nickname is all more acceptable because it also refers to other tricolours, including the francophones' cousins on the other side of the Atlantic.

But if the Canadiens have been, over one hundred years, a team with a complex identity in which have mixed freely and effectively owners, coaches, players, and fans of all origins, all languages, and all religions (the Canadiens are more in the image of the City of Montreal than in that of the Province of Quebec), why are francophone Quebecers so sure the team belongs to them? Where does this idea come from? From where have they acquired this conviction that they declare so passionately and so bombastically in terms like below?

> The Habs are not just a story of hockey. It is first of all a story of courage, sacrifice, darkness and the victory of a French-Canadian people that sometimes resembles a Gallic village. The history of the Canadiens is a source of inspiration for the French Canadians who draw on the recognition of the value, the talent and the determination of a Francophone team that built itself and wrote itself into the heart of the struggle that was tearing apart French Canadians and English Canadians. (Garand, 2009, p. 6; translation)

Quebec owes this francophone appropriation of the Canadiens to one man: Maurice Richard, obviously. He was the one who proved to Quebecers that they could beat any English Canadian, any American! "One thing remains certain: since Maurice Richard in particular, the Montreal Canadiens are in a way the national club of Quebecers" (Bérubé, 1973, p. 200; translation). The Canadiens owe this status to an event in the life of that great player, "the Maurice Richard riot" of 17 March 1955. "When Maurice Richard was suspended, every single French Canadian felt punished and angry" (Aquin and Yanacopoulo, 1972, p. 122; translation).

Outraged by the suspension of Richard for the duration of the playoffs (he had punched a linesman as a fight was being broken up), the Canadiens fans, united no matter what language they spoke, booed, insulted, and then physically attacked the man responsible for the suspension, Clarence Campbell, the commissioner of the National Hockey League, who had come to watch a game at the Forum. The Canadiens fans forced the cancellation of the game, left the Forum, and went on a rampage, first around the Forum, then on St Catherine Street in downtown Montreal.

Quebecers would come to remember this event as the moment they dared to revolt – as the beginning of the Quiet Revolution, a wake-up call for Quebec consciousness: "Some cultural observers have called *l'affair Richard* [*sic*] the flashpoint for Quebec's 'Quiet Revolution,' manifested in the 'masters in our own house' policies of Quebec governments in the 1960s as a response to 200 years of English Canadian and American domination" (McKinley, 2000, p. 189). It was very much thanks to Maurice Richard and to the riot that the Canadiens came to embody pride in being Québécois. In return, Quebec has imposed this dogma on them – "You will speak French!" – and expects them to favour Quebec players.

A Dogma of the Canadiens: "Through Suffering, You Will Win!"

In the dressing room of the Canadiens, we find the famous lines of the poem "In Flanders Fields" in its original version – "To you, from failing hands, we throw / The torch; be yours to hold it High" – and in the Canadiens' own French translation – "Nos bras meurtris vous tendent le flambeau, / À vous toujours de le porter bien haut." Chosen during the 1952–3 season by Dick Irvin (or perhaps by Frank Selke), these two lines have become the motto of the Canadiens. They have been scrupulously recopied in the club's new dressing room, in what was the Molson Centre and is now the Bell Centre.

I am unable to evaluate the real effect of a such a motto on the Canadiens players. But I can highlight the specific characteristics of the French translation of the lines. It is neither a word-for-word translation of the text by John McCrae, nor its official translation ("À vous jeunes désabusés, À vous de porter l'oriflamme").[5] Between the English and French versions, there are slight differences, and a lot of meaning can be found in these details.

The "failing hands" has become "bras meurtris" ("bruised arms"), a triple change: an extension of the hands to the arms, the change from a verb meaning failure to a verb suggesting suffering (bruise), and the shift from the active voice (failing) to the passive voice (bruised).

It is a small step from passive to Passion, a step I can easily cross in the Quebec context. The change from "failing hands" to "nos bras meurtris" (the possessive removes any doubt about who possesses those arms) takes all its meaning in the context of a Catholic Quebec. The bruised arms evoke other wounds, those of the crucified Christ, an image that is central in all Catholic churches. And they refer to a very common expression in Quebec: "nous sommes nés pour un petit pain," "we are born for a small crust of bread," by which Quebecers express the small share that the anglophones left them for a long time, and consequently, the little ambition they set for themselves. The motto of the Canadiens corresponds precisely to this doloristic mentality in Quebec.

But at the same time, it transcends that expression, because the Canadiens allowed Quebec to hope for much more than a small crust of bread, a big loaf, a brioche, the whole bakery! The Canadiens have won twenty-four Stanley Cups, more than any other hockey club, and this has made them the second most victorious sports organization in North America (after the New York Yankees). By declaring in the French version that "the torch" – here certainly pride, the capacity to win, and the responsibility to be part of the Canadiens – is held by bruised arms, the Canadiens recall that Quebec can win, even though it is through inevitable suffering.

Not My Religion

After presenting as honestly as possible the facts that permit me to talk about the Canadiens as a religion, I can firmly state that the religion of the Canadiens is not *my* religion, that the God of the religion of the Canadiens is not *my* God. I will give three reasons for this.

First of all, the religion of the Canadiens is too fragile. We tend to forget that the Canadiens have existed only since the last century. That is certainly a long time for a hockey team. And it is certainly respectable for any sports team in North America. But for a religion, it is a short time! The future of the Canadiens is not guaranteed, and neither is that of the religion of the Canadiens. Of course, their special status (they are the oldest of the NHL's original six teams, the only francophone team, etc.) protects them. But when money is involved, anything is possible and feelings come second. Even the Canadiens could be sold and moved to another city. As strange as it may seem in the Quebec of today, where the religion of the Canadiens seems much more fashionable than Christianity, I am ready to wager that Christianity will last longer than the Canadiens.

Second, the religion of the Canadiens is too tribal. It succumbs easily to the danger of monopolizing a God as only the God of the Habs. It implies almost inevitably the denigration of the teams against which the Canadiens play. It requires hating the cities those opposing teams represent, too often insulting their fans, and sometimes (fortunately rarely) attacking them physically. The God I believe in promotes love, not hate.

And finally, third, the religion of the Canadiens is too selective. Beyond its unifying image, the Canadiens are a veritable machine for producing selection, for producing exclusion, on the ice and in the stands. On the ice, it selects according to talent. It forms the summit of a hockey pyramid, which keeps only the exceptional players and pitilessly eliminates those who are mediocre or only good. And with respect to the stands, it selects there too, but according to money, reserving the best seats for the wealthiest or for those who are prepared to spend the most. My religion operates on a radically different principle. It is a religion of choosing in which God does not reward people according to their merits; instead, He freely welcomes certain persons or certain peoples – I would say *all* persons and *all* peoples – without concern for their wealth, their talent, their behaviour, or even their faith. This no doubt unfair, but it's the only way to compensate for natural or cultural inequalities. It is obvious that the Canadiens would not survive for long if they applied that principle. And that is why they can't be my religion, why they cannot give meaning to my life.

The NHL can, however, seem less selective, favouring the less strong teams (through the draft system) or the less wealthy (by establishing a salary cap). But there is nothing generous in this. These equalization measures have only one objective, which is to make the season more interesting so as to increase media coverage and thereby generate more money. In my opinion, a religion in which the key goal is winning games and making money is a bad religion.

The Line between Faith and Idolatry

As theologian Daniel Lys used to say, there are two kinds of idolatry. There is the idolatry of someone who worships a false god, but there is also the idolatry of someone who worships the true God in a false manner. Without any doubt, we find both forms of idolatry in the religion of the Canadiens. To put it succinctly, Théodore worships a false God, while Victoria worships the true God, but falsely. But the fact that the religion of the Canadiens is idolatry still does not condemn it. Put in its proper place, provided you make nothing more of it than what it is, the Canadiens can sustain the faith of believers.

May God Be with the Canadiens!

Théodore has made the Canadiens the object of his religion. His worship is for the team. He puts his trust in it. And that is why his way belongs to the first form of idolatry: worship of a false god. And I can prove it! But to do this, I have to introduce a little of my Protestant theology.

For me, it is more than a conviction, it is a certainty: God is revealed not only on Sunday in church; he can also be revealed on Friday in the mosque, on Saturday in the synagogue, every day, everywhere, and obviously on Tuesday nights at the Bell Centre. From the same perspective, I believe that God does not reveal himself solely through priests, pastors, rabbis, or imams; he can reveal himself through *anyone*, including a hockey player. And I believe that God reveals himself not only in theological concepts, or in religious expressions, or in music, liturgies, sacraments, or sacred objects; he can also be revealed – if he wishes – in all words, all songs, all rituals, including those of a game of the Canadiens, and in all objects, including a hockey stick.[6]

For example, "the Church" (any Church) is only one means available to God to enter into a relationship with human beings. And this relationship can be formed directly with an individual or through a cultural artefact other than a Church (a Church is obviously a cultural artifact) such as a song, a person, a film, or a gesture.

Moreover, this concept is based on a theology with a double-inspiration. God, through his spirit, inspires the person who produces an artefact so that it becomes a word of God, an image of God, a taste of God, and so on. But God also inspires the person who perceives the artefact so that it becomes, for that person, a word of God, an image of God, a taste of God, and so on.

Like all cultural artefacts, a beautiful goal by Max Pacioretty, a magnificent stop by Carey Price, or a solid check by P.K. Subban are all capable of carrying the revelation of God, as long as the person who sees them is capable of perceiving them as a foretaste of the beauty, perfection, and pleasure that will become complete and common in the Kingdom of God, when we are all capable of scoring like Pacioretty, stopping pucks like Price, and defending like Subban. A beautiful goal by Pacioretty can transmit the revelation of God for the one to whom He gives an understanding as a sign of this harmony that He wants for all of us. A beautiful goal by Pacioretty works as a sign of the penetration of the Kingdom of God into daily life, like a miracle that shows the power of God and His love for the world.

So for me, it is obvious that a beautiful goal by Pacioretty can function as a religious artefact, suitable for revealing God to someone who has eyes to see and who knows how to use them. But on one condition, which is to consider Pacioretty not as a God but as a *message* from God, a kind of angel, according to the traditional term. For the Canadiens to be capable of revealing God, it is necessary for the team to give up on being a religion, for it to accept being what it is, a hockey club.

This distinction is essential because there is always a risk of giving Pacioretty (or any other player) all the credit for the beautiful goal and to consider him as a superior being endowed with supernatural powers, which is precisely what a theologian would call an idol. Félix Leclerc, for example, yielded to this temptation when he wrote on 19 October 1983 about Maurice Richard: "When he shoots, America screams. When he scores, the deaf hear. When he is penalized, the telephone lines heat up. When he passes, the rookies dream. It's the wind skating. It's all of Quebec on its feet" (quoted in Pellerin, 1988, p. 11; translation).

Of course, this is how the Canadiens can become a religion, a religion that I, as a Protestant theologian, would consider idolatry. But idolatry is not an inevitability. A beautiful goal by Pacioretty can also serve to *strengthen* faith. "It is customary in Protestant theology to analyze the performance of a man, his *Leistung*, as Martin Luther said, from the perspective of justification through faith. Any performance, from this perspective, can be transformed either into self-justification and idolatry, or into human achievement aware of its limitations and its relationship with God" (Müller, 2008, p. 45; translation). When a believer includes the Canadiens within the framework of justification through faith, when he or she relates Pacioretty's beautiful goal to God, not to the player himself, and not to a God who pushed the puck in the goal, but to a God who makes Pacioretty capable of scoring extraordinary goals, when the believer understands such perfection as a foretaste of what awaits us, awaits us all, in the Kingdom of God, then the Canadiens begin to transmit the revelation of God.

That makes all the difference. And it is because he does not do this that Théodore is wrong and that his way is idolatry. The Canadiens represent an opportunity to meet God if, and only if, the team is not considered to be a God and, of course, if it does not take itself to be God. It is when the fans view the Canadiens as a cultural artefact, when they consider the players as highly talented human beings, that the Canadiens can fulfil for them a religious function and bring them into a relationship with God. And it is perhaps after a defeat that we can most easily verify whether the Canadiens are a religion or a cultural artefact. The fans love winners, and they love winning teams. The fans of the Canadiens are sure that God is with the team when they win. They even perceive their victories as a demonstration that God loves the Canadiens. But how do they deal with defeat? They often perceive it as a sign that God has abandoned them. In my opinion, they are wrong. They should learn that God is also, and perhaps especially, with the Habs in difficult times, the evenings of defeat and elimination. If they doubt this, they should remember that Christianity is based on a loser, on a defeat. The man who dies alone and miserable on a cross is the one who shows the true face of God.

So, yes, a beautiful goal by Pacioretty is a foretaste of the Kingdom of God, because ordinary things can carry the revelation of God, can be parables or metaphors to describe the ultimate reality. Even a lucky goal, a chance goal, a "garbage goal," is a foretaste of the Kingdom of God, but the advantage of a beautiful goal is that the goalie is not to blame. And who knows, if Jesus had been a Quebecer, perhaps he would have imagined a parable like this: "The Kingdom of God is like a beautiful Pacioretty goal. The fan who recorded it invites his friends to see it and watch it over and over again ..."

May God Bless the Habs!

Victoria's way exemplifies the second form of idolatry: false worship of the true God. Victoria does not make the same mistake as Théodore. She does not worship the Canadiens – she merely asks God for help. Nevertheless, Victoria's way is idolatry. Here again, I can demonstrate it by presenting another aspect of my Protestant theology.

I have no difficulty, even as a Protestant, Western academic theologian, stating that God takes an interest in the Canadiens and that he can intervene in lives of the Canadiens or in the games of the Canadiens. God can help the owner and the general manager run the organization.

He can help the coach train his team. He can help the players play. He can help the medical team provide care, and help the support staff with getting the equipment ready and cleaning the ice. He can help the fans cheer the team on. Some believers or some non-believers might consider it nonsensical to think that God could take an interest in the Canadiens. I admit there are more important things in the world, but that does not mean that God could not or should not take an interest in the Canadiens. There are at least three reasons for this.

First of all, even though a victory or a defeat of the Canadiens does not change the face of the world, it can have a big impact, at least in Montreal and in Quebec. To be convinced of this, simply consider the issues related to the Canadiens: the money they generate, the jobs they create, the injuries they cause, the more or less crazy dreams they generate, the hopes and despair they inspire. For all of these reasons, for both the positive and the negative, the Habs need God's help.

Second, God's interest in the Canadiens does not come at the expense of other situations or other people who might have a more urgent or more crucial need for God's help. The God I believe in is versatile, multitasking – in more traditional terms, He is omnipotent. He is capable of intervening at the same time and with the same effectiveness inside the Bell Centre and in any church, in any hospital, and in any gesture of love. Need I add that God has exactly the same interest in the Canadiens as He has in all the other teams of the NHL? Whatever the fans of the Canadiens might think, God also blesses the Leafs, the Bruins, the Penguins, and even the Flyers; God intervenes for the Canadiens, and he also intervenes for their adversaries.

Finally, I refuse to decide myself what God should take an interest in, what he should take care of. I am incapable of placing limits on God's actions. What is enough for God to be concerned about? What would be too trivial for him to take an interest in it? I think it is wiser to let God decide, even though, for my part, I would submit that everything is important in his eyes and that nothing is too trivial for him.

So I have no reason to think there is any place in the world where human activity escapes the interest of God – not even a hockey game. But I would like to be even more specific about the form taken by the help God can give the Canadiens.

Let us imagine first of all that he intervenes directly. A fatalist would say that everything that happens to the Canadiens, good or bad, depends on the will of God. But believing in such direct intervention by God in all aspects of the lives of the Canadiens would force me to thank him whenever a player is injured or a Canadiens player injures a rival player. I should consider these occurrences – objectively, they are bad things – as the will of God to punish bad behaviour (e.g., a player who has played badly or who has missed a match), or to rebalance a game when a team is too strong, or to make room for a substitute player or a young player. I know that God sometimes works in mysterious ways, but for Him to act in such a way would, in my eyes, be very strange.

Again from the perspective of His direct intervention, I cannot believe either that God could deflect a shot to go straight into an empty net. When such an incident occurs, my reason and my faith would cause me instead to eliminate all supernatural causes, such as divine or diabolical intervention, and prefer a natural explanation such as a small bump on the ice. I would attribute a less obvious unforeseen occurrence – a shot hitting the post, for example – to clumsiness or bad luck.

But I do not conclude that God does not play a role in lives of the Canadiens. I believe rather in the possibility of indirect intervention by God, on the ice and outside the rink. I believe that God intervenes indirectly, through those who do His will. There is a famous saying: "God has no other hands but ours." In applying that phrase to hockey, I would say that God has no other hands but those of the players to handle the puck or to stop it. He has no other brain but the brain of the coach to come up with plays. He has no other voices but those of the fans to cheer on a team.

I believe that God helps the players who recognize they need His help. And I was strengthened in my conviction when I heard the testimony of Daniel Bouchard, a former goalie with Quebec Nordiques, who converted to Christianity and whose nickname was "the hand of God." In 1982, he declared on the evening of a victory, coming off the ice still dripping with sweat: "I praise God because he made stops for me. I felt I was just a tool for him. I'd prayed enough. Sometimes it doesn't work!" (Desrosiers and Thibault, 2009). The fact that he said "God made stops for me" could lead you to think that he believed that God had intervened directly in front of the net. But the goalie added a clarification, which made all the difference: "I felt I was just a tool for him." Everything becomes clear. It was not God who blocked the puck, but Daniel Bouchard, in fact. Since God has no hands, He needed the hand of a man to stop the shots. That evening, the hand of God was Bouchard's left hand. That evening, God used Bouchard's hand as a tool.

God can help any hockey team, even the Canadiens. But He does not handle the puck Himself. He acts indirectly, by inspiring the owners and general managers, the players and the fans. It is therefore not God who makes the puck skip or deflect. He is not the one who makes it roll for one or the other of the teams. God does not act, but He can inspire the player who is handling the puck, the person who made the stick or the puck, the person who cleaned the ice surface – all things that influence the trajectory of the puck.

I can now come back to Victoria's way and explain why that way is idolatry. It is clearly a case, I repeat, of the second form of idolatry, since Victoria practises false worship of the true God. It seems to me, however, that asking for help from Brother André could be seen as first a form of idolatry. Because if Victoria adores Brother André, or if it is him she is counting on, she is definitely worshipping a false god. But perhaps she is avoiding that form of idolatry. Perhaps she knows that without God, Brother André by himself can do nothing, that all his power comes from God. Perhaps she understands that asking for help from Brother André means asking for God's help. I hope so, even though her mom's e-mail never mentions God but only Brother André, eight times. As a Protestant theologian, I cannot help thinking that she would have been better to ask God directly for help. That would be the best way to avoid any risk of the first form of idolatry, even though it it would not automatically avert the dangers of the second.

But Victoria's way obviously belongs to that second form of idolatry. Victoria is wrong, because she believes that direct intervention is compulsory or automatic as long as you have the necessary faith ("but she's the kind who quickly gets favours from Heaven") to accomplish good deeds (Victoria had "distributed medals and statuettes of Brother André to each of her classmates) or to say the right prayers (the mom suggests that her daughter "ask for help from Brother André"). Even if Victoria worships the true God (of which I am still doubtful), her way is still idolatry because she worships him in a false way. God's intervention can never be automatic or compulsory. It is always the result of a freely taken decision. No act of piety, as profound as it may be, can change the course of a game or a season. Better, then, if Victoria had prayed for the players to agree to become instruments of God.

A Fish in the Logo

I will conclude this chapter with a short meditation, one that resembles a children's game: "Who will help Olivier find the blue fish in the logo of the Canadiens?" Take a few seconds to look at the logo and try to find the fish. It is there, I can assure you. It is swimming somewhere within the design. To make it visible, you just have to ignore the big letter C, delete the two small blue squares, and complete the inner blue line. Do you see it now? Once you have spotted it, it is obvious.

Everyone knows what the fish symbol means. It is often seen on the back of cars. Without any doubt, it is a Christian symbol. In fact, it was one of the very first, a symbol used long before the symbol of the cross, a symbol that was found in the catacombs. The fish was and remains a Christian symbol because its name in Greek, *ichtus*, is the acronym of a confession of faith. Spelled *I–C–H–T–U–S*, it evoked the initials of five Greek words: Jesus Christ, Son of God, Saviour.

In the first centuries of our era, the fish (the word and the image) was used by Christians as a code, a secret code because Christians were persecuted. They needed to be able to recognize one another without their enemies identifying them. The symbol of the fish gradually fell out of use, supplanted by the cross, especially when Christianity became the religion of the Roman Empire and Christians no longer needed to hide. The symbol almost disappeared entirely until it was revived by the Christian Evangelicals at the beginning of the twentieth century. They made it the sign of their faith.

But what can we say about the fish in the logo of the Canadiens? Could it represent a subliminal confession of faith? Would it be discreet evidence of the club's Christianity? Of course not! But writing that is not enough. We have to remember the theology of double-inspiration. It matters little whether the fish in the logo is accidental, it matters little that it has no deliberate Christian meaning. I see that fish in the logo. And for me, it takes on a theological value, a Christian value. For me, it has the status of a confession of Christian faith. And for you too now, I hope. Now, you will no longer be able to look at that logo in the same way. Every time you see it, you will also see the blue fish and you will remember that Jesus is Christ, the Son of God, the Saviour. Which seems me to be a good way of putting a little faith, not religion, into the Canadiens. Permit me to call it immodestly Olivier's way ...

NOTES

1 This chapter is based on the presentation titled "Habs' Passion: On the Thin Red Line between Faith and Idolatry," presented at the conference "Hockey on the Border: An International Scholarly Conference," in

Buffalo, on 4 June 2010 and at the "Summer Literary Seminars," in Montreal, on 22 June 2010. It was published in Olivier Bauer, *Hockey as a Religion: The Montreal Canadiens* (Common Ground, 2011).

2 "Religion," in the *Encyclopedia Britannica Online*, www.britannica.com. My emphasis.

3 Patrick Roy, "NHL – 1 on 1 with Patrick Roy." Interview on the TSN network with Ray Ferraro, 22 November 2008.

4 Entry by "sd2smith," 3 December 2008, in the comments section of the article "Worshipping les Canadiens," CBCsports.ca.

5 Veterans Affairs Canada, http://www.veterans.gc.ca/.

6 For more information on this concept, see Bauer (2007).

3 We Are Habs and Normative

NICOLAS MOREAU AND CHLOÉ NAHAS

In this brief chapter, "Le Grand Club" itself is not the main topic of our discussion. Rather, the Montreal Canadiens are a methodology – or, to be more precise, material for analysis. Our focus here is in fact on a complex subject in current sociology: the social characteristics of the individual. What defines the individual in the contemporary Western world? What are the requirements today? What are the vectors by which individuals should orient their conduct and behaviours? These are the questions that concern us here.

In liberal societies such as ours, it is sometimes difficult to identify social norms directly since they are so implicit, multifaceted, or contradictory, or so ingrained that they seem "natural." However, doing this work of explaining social norms is essential, because understanding them allows us to comprehend the social grammar, in other words the way in which society communicates with itself and with its members. Two methodological choices can be applied in order to carry out this work of explication.

The first possibility would be to analyse the characteristics of the individual "by default" (Castel and Haroche, 2001, pp. 107–161; translation), since the individual, in his or her potential "deviance," shows us what you cannot do and therefore, conversely, indicates what is socially desirable. The second methodological possibility – our theoretical framework – results from the analysis of an individual "by excess" (to borrow from the terminology of Robert Castel) in order to understand everyday social demands. The symbol, even the quintessence, of that *superindividual* is reflected perfectly in sports icons. In France in the 1980s, "champion athletes became symbols of social excellence while earlier they were rather the sign of the backwardness of the people" (Ehrenberg, 1991, p. 14; translation); it seems different in Quebec, where, for example, Maurice Richard (to cite one example) became the symbol and the glory of French Canadians starting in the 1940s. Thus sport – in Quebec, more specifically hockey – is an highly relevant normative laboratory for the social world. This is because our demands on athletes amount to a kind of magnifying mirror that reflects what we want to be and what is asked of us every day.

The Athlete as a Normative Ideal

The high-profile athlete is the "vector of a social idealization" (Queval, 2004, p. 204; translation). But he is not essentially different from the lambda individual, as Paul Yonnet thinks, for whom "the champion is a monster, an extraordinary individual, someone hard to imagine for ordinary mortals" (Yonnet, 1998, p. 203; translation). This qualitative split between the sports icon and "ordinary mortals" seems to us to be epistemologically invalid, since the figure of the high-profile athlete crystallizes contemporary social normalcy. In fact, the athlete is a normative fantasy in a society where the regulation of behaviours is based more and more on possibility (Am I capable of doing it?) and less and less on strict obedience to rules (What am I permitted to do?) (Ehrenberg, 1998). The champion is therefore no longer Yonnet's monster. Between him and the average individual (in the statistical sense of the term), the only difference is quantitative, in the sense that the athlete embodies a normative extreme, a positive deviation from the statistical average.

So we propose to analyse the qualities attributed to (or required of) the players of the Montreal Canadiens in order to better understand contemporary social norms – in other words, what is asked of us (implicitly and explicitly) every day. It is not our goal to examine the workings of the world of hockey, but rather to use that world as a means, an interface, a epistemologically valid tool for attempting to understand facets of the contemporary Western individual.

The dialectic between sport and society takes on a dimension in Quebec that, if not exceptional, is at least distinct, for the Montreal Canadiens are, to borrow the slogan of FC Barcelona, "més que un club" (more than a club).[1] Some of the "glorieux" have played a decisive role in civil society. That said, through his own writings, Maurice Richard played a *direct* role in the affirmation of French Canadians, in particular when he stood up for Bernard "Boom-Boom" Geoffrion when he was suspended (Melançon, 2008). Beyond the French fact, the Montreal Canadiens and its icons are images of what we are. Whether they are doing well or badly, we always care about them because, sociologically, they are our mirror.

Methodological Aspects

To analyse the qualities required, demanded, praised, or lacking in the Canadiens players, we proceeded as follows. We selected all the articles in the French-language Montreal daily *La Presse* published from the first day (15 April) to the last day (24 May) of the 2010 playoffs in which the headlines contained the family name of one of the players who played during the first three rounds (participation in a minimum of one game). We then divided the articles into three major categories: goalies, defencemen, and forwards. Of the articles analysed, 26 mentioned goalies (Price and Halak), 26, defencemen (Gill, Gorges, Hamrlik, Markov, O'Byrne, Spacek, Subban, and Bergeron), and 46, forwards (Cammalleri, Darche, Gionta, Gomez, Kostitsyn [Andrei and Sergei], Lapierre, Maxwell, Moen, Plekanec, Pouliot, Pyatt, Metropolit, and Moore). The characteristics of players could come either from the words of journalists or the coach, or from one of the players themselves as they described their practice (or that of their teammate), and they were analysed without distinguishing one source from the other. For each of the categories (goalies, defencemen, forwards), we took the three dimensions most frequently mentioned, dimensions that emerged following a series of codifications and classifications.

When the article's headline mentioned the name of only one player, only the characteristics related to that player were used in the analysis. When the article's headline included the names of several players, two choices were possible, depending on the category those players belonged to. For example, if the players mentioned in the headline belonged to the same category, all of the characteristics attributed to those players were selected and analysed. When several categories were present in the headline, the attributes of each player were analysed according to their category. We would like to mention, to conclude, that the articles were content-analysed – more specifically, they were analysed by categorical theme.

The Performance and the Strength of Character of the Goalie: The Need for a Rare Gem

The first dimension, the characteristics of goalies, is related to their performance, which can be defined simply by the difference between the number of saves and the number of shots on goal:

> While the Canadiens were able to maximize their chances at one end of the rink, Jaroslav Halak did his part at the other end. He stopped fifteen shots from the Caps in the first period, including some big saves at the expense of Joe Corvo and Alexander Semin. ("Le Canadien tient promesse. Jaroslav Halak réalise 37 arrêts et mène le CH à une victoire de 2–1" ["The Canadiens Keep Their Promise: Jaroslav Halak Makes 37 Saves and Leads the Habs to a 2–1 Victory"]). (24 April, p. 2; translation)

> "When a goalie excels this way, we try to place the puck in a very small space. However, on our only goal, we simply shot the puck toward the net in order to redirect the direction of the play. Okay, you could say that we missed a few chances, but on the whole, you have to say that Halak was exceptional," explained Boudreau. ("Halak était dans une bulle" ["Halak Was in a Bubble"]) (27 April, p. 4; translation)

> The last time that the Canadiens played at the Bell Centre, Jaroslav Halak gave the performance of his life with 53 stops against the Washington Capitals in the sixth game of the series ... A week later, the Tricolore is still in the running, thanks in particular to the brilliance of the Slovak goalie. ("Tous derrière Halak" ["All behind Halak"]) (4 May, p. 7; translation)

The second dimension is related to being unique, standing out from one's peers:

> The Canadiens' goalie, first class in the regular season, brought his play against the Washington Capitals to the level of the great goalies in the history of the NHL. ("Sans Halak, point de salut" ["No Salvation without Halak"]) (30 April, p. 1; translation)

> But for the former goalie coach of the Habs, what Jaroslav Halak accomplished in the series between the Canadiens and the Capitals was unique. "He played with almost inhuman skill in the first match and the three

> latest victories," he said yesterday. ("Halak a été presque inhumain" ["Halak Was Almost Inhuman") (30 April, p. 4; translation)

The third dimension is strength of character, "mental toughness":

> Standing in front of his locker, Price sympathized with Halak. "It's frustrating to any goalie to get taken out of a game," he said. "But Jaro's greatest quality is that he's mentally strong. He maintains his confidence." ("Douze minutes nous ont coûté le match. Martin n'a pas prisé le manque de discipline de Gomez et a défendu Halak" ["Twelve Minutes Cost Us the Game: Martin Did Not Appreciate Gomez's Lack of Discipline and Defended Halak") (20 April, p. 2; translation)

> They are no doubt right if we limit ourselves to the physique and technique of the young man. But when we take into account "mental toughness," it's another story. ("Halak n'aura pas ce qu'il mérite" ["Halak Will Not Get What He Deserves"]) (8 May, p. 4; translation)

The Work Ethic of Defencemen

The capacity to make a difference – in other words, to have a direct impact on the outcome of the game – is one of the dimensions that emerged during the analysis of this category of players:

> Roman Hamrlik's mistake that led to the second goal of the Capitals was still fresh in everyone's memory, yesterday, before the departure of the Canadiens to Washington. Because it is the symbol of what makes the difference in this series ("Martin: 'Hamrlik peut nous en donner plus'" ["Martin: 'Hamrlik Can Give Us More'"]) (23 April, p. 2; translation)

> It was still only Subban's sixth game in the NHL and he scored one goal out of five ... "I'm impressed," admitted Michael Cammalleri. "He's a big help to our team " ("P.K. Subban, un baume sur la défense" ("P.K. Subban, a Relief on Defence"]) (3 May, p. 4; translation)

The second dimension for the defencemen is physical commitment:

> "Hal is built for the playoffs or the playoffs are made for Hal," described his partner Josh Gorges. "The hockey currently being played is his. It's intense, physical, tough. Not surprising that he's at the top of his form."

> ("Hal Gill: personnage central d'un scénario surprenant" ["Hal Gill: Central Character in a Surprising Scenario"]) (30 April, p. 1; translation)

> "It's nice to see him so engaged," Hal Gill mentioned. "He gets into things, he's aggressive, he makes plays, he skates and he's strong" ("P.K. Subban, un baume sur la défense" ["P.K. Subban, a Relief on Defence"]) (3 May, p. 4; translation)

The third dimension is being responsible, since an error can create a direct scoring chance for the opposing team:

> I want to play my game, be responsible defensively and not give too much to the other team," he explained. "Scoring a goal was a bonus" ("'J'ai été une inspiration pour moi-même.' Aider le CH à remporter le match était tout un accomplissement pour Jaroslav Spacek ["'I was an inspiration for myself': Helping the Habs Win the Game Was Quite an Achievement for Jaroslav Spacek"]). (11 May, p. 3; translation)

The Forwards: Between Pleasure and Commitment to the Team

An important dimension of our corpus was, especially for the forwards, the pleasure related to the game or to participation in the playoffs:

> "From the beginning of the playoffs, I had a lot of fun coming to the arena in the morning," he admitted. "I had some very tough times during the year." ("Lapierre: 'Je penserai à ce but-là ce soir'" ["Lapierre: 'I Will Think About That Goal Tonight'"]) (11 May, p. 3; translation)

> Cammalleri himself is not ready to say that he is developing a *money player* side. It is mostly pleasure that motivates him now. "Last year, it was my first playoffs and I was probably too nervous, too wound up," he explained. "But I was really excited about returning to the playoffs. And that was a factor in my decision, last summer, to join a team that had a chance of going to the playoffs." ("Cammalleri cherche à contrôler ses émotions" ["Cammalleri Tries to Control His Emotions"]) (12 May, p. 4; translation)

Among the forwards, hard work also stood out:

> "I worked very hard with the doctors and therapists to speed up my return to the game. I worked hard in the gym and on the stationary bike.

> I suffered to get back into shape, but it hurt even more watching the games from up high in the press box. We are in the playoffs, I fought all season to keep my position and help this team win and I'd finally have the chance to play," said Metropolit after morning practice yesterday ("Metropolit fait mentir les médecins: 'Ça faisait plus mal de suivre les matchs d'en haut ...'" ["Metropolit Defies the Doctors: 'It Hurt More Following the Games from Up High ...'"]) (20 April, p. 4; translation)

> "I work hard in the practices and off the ice, and the guys see it," Lapierre stated. ("Lapierre: 'J'ai accepté mon rôle'" ["Lapierre: 'I Accepted My Role'"]) (12 May, p. 3; translation)

The third dimension among the forwards was commitment, either towards the sport (hockey in this case) or towards their team:

> "I think that not scoring more goals during the season created frustration for him," suggested the coach. "But for the time being, what is most important is his commitment to the team." ("Pourquoi Lapierre a retrouvé sa vitesse" ["Why Lapierre Got up to Speed"]) (7 May, p. 4; translation)

> Not only did he clobber defenceman Alex Goligoski [...], but his involvement in all facets of the game makes him a changed player compared to the regular season. "Even if he had some tough times that season, you can see that he's devoted to hockey," Jacques Martin said. "And it's always good to see a player who's really devoted to hockey, because that's a sentiment that you can build on. ("Lapierre: 'J'ai accepté mon rôle'" ["Lapierre: 'I Accepted My Role'"]) (12 May, p. 3; translation)

What do these characteristics tell us about the society in which we live?[2] How are the virtues attributed to the Montreal Canadiens players indicative of our lifestyles? Keeping these questions in mind as a common thread, we will now discuss the results.

Performance as Social Engine

When they express themselves in the public sphere, the various experts on the question are nearly unanimous in saying that contemporary Western societies are permeated with the idea of performance standards. It seems that the quintessence of the social reality experienced by many of us is the figure of the high-profile athlete. Is the demand for performance standards really a new phenomenon? In the sports world, certainly not, since the essence of competitive sport resides in that principle, notwithstanding Baron de Coubertin's desire to make participation the sporting ideal.

Let us ask the question with respect to the social world: Is performance characteristic of a contemporary form of individuality? To answer this question, we will borrow the words of Alain Ehrenberg, according to whom performance, since the 1980s, has occupied a unique place in Western societies (Ehrenberg, 1991, pp. 13–22). In other words, while performance has always existed (in various forms and under many names), these days it is at the centre of our preoccupations. One hypothesis that can take into account this inflation in semantics and in practice is precisely the shift towards a so-called liberal society, that is, one in which traditional norms of discipline and obedience have a much less important place than before. The shift from "what is permitted" to "what I am capable of" opened the way for the performance society.

In a disciplinary society (to borrow Foucault's term), the boundary between functionality and performance seems to us to be very thin, since performing effectively can be summed up, one might say, as simply doing what is formally asked of us. This is also the case for functionality. Thus, performance and functionality are almost interchangeable. However, in a society governed by more flexible norms, as contemporary Western societies can be, performance and functionality are more and more distinct. For example, performance regulates more the behaviours of subjects (and makes distinctions), since what is asked is much more fluid and flexible and therefore permits a normative game that is more complex and more open. For example, in a factory, a worker on an assembly line is functional; if not, he is replaced. The boundary between functionality and performance, if it exists, is porous. The situation is more complex for the contemporary senior manager; because what is asked of him is less defined, he can play with the rules of game, go beyond them, and so on. In other words, being less prescriptive and giving employees more freedom has made it possible to augment the criteria of performance.

Being the Hero of One's Banality

Being unique, being oneself, is today a very meaningful normative injunction. Like Halak, who was able, through his miraculous saves, to become an exceptional player in the hearts of Canadiens fans, we have to write our own story each day. We are normatively inclined to be the heroes of our own stories, however banal they are and whatever social world we belong to. Examples are numerous. Think of the inflation of biographies in contemporary literature and on reality TV. Personal accounts in their various forms are very fashionable and are also part of this phenomenon. In short, every story is interesting, because it is unique. It is legitimate because it is our own.

The need to be unique is characteristic of the new social normativity. It regulates our behaviours in a number of areas, such as work, where the employer will ask the job candidate not whether he possesses the abilities to occupy the position, but rather what he can contribute to the company as an individual, being unique and exceptional (Ehrenreich, 2005). This norm of being one's own hero should, in our view, be looked at alongside the end of the great narratives, the societal metanarratives (Lyotard, 1984, xxiv–xxv). Indeed, heroic figures, Bible stories, even some scientific theories seem to have been symbolically replaced by individual narrations that are each as ordinary as the next. We have to be normatively unique, and no one is immune from that.

An Emotional Society

The management of emotions has taken up a predominant place in contemporary Western societies. Popular psychology books are a striking example of this, as is the omnipresence of psychologists in the media to comment on all kinds of social phenomena (consequences of the economic crisis, the personality of a killer, changes in how we live as couples, etc.). This emergence of the society of emotions, like performance, can be related to the end of the so-called disciplinary society:

> In business, the disciplinary models (Taylorist and Fordist) of human resources management have given way to norms that encourage staff to adopt autonomous behaviours, including those low in the hierarchy ... The fashions of regulation and domination of labour are based less on mechanical obedience than on initiative: responsibility, ability to develop, to make plans, motivation, flexibility, etc., constitute a new managerial liturgy. The constraint imposed on the worker is no longer the man-machine of repetitive work, but the entrepreneur of flexible work ... It is less a matter of subjugating bodies than of mobilizing the affects and mental abilities of each employee. (Ehrenberg, 1998, p. 234; translation)

For example, in a society regulated more around norms of initiative, responsibility, flexibility, and the ability to act on one's own, it seems to us that the mental aspects have become essential. To be more precise, we think that the social normativity inherent in liberal societies has generically weakened the individual, who is therefore more prone to mental health disorders. In other words, the mental cost of functioning in society is higher. We agree here with the hypothesis of Sennett, for whom the absence of a more or less stable future results for the individual in a "corrosion of character" (Sennett, 1998), and Ehrenberg's vision, which attributes, in part, depressive disorders to the weight of possibilities: "The rise of depression has highlighted the tensions produced by this confrontation, as the realm of the permitted crumbles before the onslaught of the possible" (Ehrenberg, 1998, p. 290; translation).

From that point on, if the individuals fabricated by the contemporary social world are generically more fragile (given that they have to be themselves, autonomous, etc., relying less and less on social institutions and more and more on their inner resources), it is hardly surprising that the management of emotions has become a pet subject in our societies.

From the Capacity to Make a Difference to Individual Accountability

The capacity to *make a difference* refers quite directly to performance and will therefore not be the object of a detailed analysis in this book. Nevertheless, this requirement of performance and distinction should be understood by taking into account the contemporary normative space and, more specifically, responsibility, which constitutes more fertile ground for this normative act and thus gives it quite considerable weight. In fact, if the individual were not capable of meeting the various social demands (or going beyond them), he would be at fault: it would mean he had not made the correct decisions (Moreau, 2009).

Wacquant (2004) spoke about the end of "sociological excuses" marked by making the individual excessively accountable. Everything happens as if everyone is responsible for his or her successes and failures. In this context, social structures can no longer be used to account for social behaviours. *Players have to make the right decisions on the ice. They are the ones primarily responsible for their fate.* This perspective, typical in sports (individual or team), has never before been so representative of the contemporary social world. The best-selling book *The Secret*, by Rhonda Byrne, contains many examples of this tendency to believe that the individual has the power to decide everything. For example, poverty in the world is said to be the result not of structural causes (even partly), but instead of the bad management of the thoughts and emotions by a large part of the population, who have within themselves all the resources they need to change their situation! This reflection by speaker Bob Proctor, followed by Byrne's explanation, would be very funny if it were not dangerous:

> Why do you think that 1 percent of the population earns around 96 percent of all the money that's being earned? Do you think that's an accident? It's designed that way. They understand something. They understand The Secret, and now you are being introduced to The Secret.
>
> People who have drawn wealth into their lives used The Secret, whether consciously or unconsciously. They think thoughts of abundance and wealth, and they do not allow any contradictory thoughts to take root in their minds. Their predominant thoughts are of wealth. They only *know* wealth, and nothing else exists in their minds. Whether they are aware of it or not, their predominant thoughts of wealth are what brought wealth to them. It is the law of attraction in action. (Byrne, 2006, p. 6; emphasis added)

Pleasure, Hard Work, and Commitment

Pleasure appeared as an essential dimension among the forwards. The pleasure of the game, of being in the playoffs, or of playing in and for Montreal. This concept of pleasure should be understood in the context of a post-disciplinary society in which personal fulfilment and hedonism have taken on considerable importance (Sennett, 1977). Thus, all areas of social life are supposed to be sources of pleasure. Most of our actions have to include some sort of enjoyment to be legitimate, and this is true even for work, which today is supposed to be a source of fulfilment, even of happiness!

This norm of pleasure leads us to the norms of hard work and commitment, which we could classify under the concept of subjective investment. For example, individuals are now asked to commit subjectively to the company, and the company is supposed to be for the individual a kind of second family. Workers are expected to love, recognize themselves in, be fulfilled by, and be concerned about the well-being of their company; indeed, their well-being and fulfilment both depend on it.

This concept of subjective investment has been steadily increasing in importance in contemporary managerial techniques to become today one of their mainstays (Laurin-Lamothe, 2011). While it is still *normal* (in the Foucauldian sense of the term, i.e., as the statistically most common behaviour), subjective investment nevertheless creates problems in a society in which occupational stability has become almost a fantasy (Sennett, 1998, p. 23). How can you ask workers, or professional athletes, to identify with their employer if they have no way of knowing, in the medium or long term, whether they will remain part of that organization? Mental health professionals would ask to their patients to be detached and to distance themselves from a shifting structure. The manager asks precisely the opposite – for workers to immerse themselves body and soul in the uncertainty.

Limitations

It goes without saying that this essay has certain limitations. The playoffs likely differ from the regular season. We have, for example, reviewed many articles on the performance of goalies, especially Halak's performance. That year, it has to be acknowledged, his was beyond exceptional. Is not this large number of articles on the Slovak goalie of the Canadiens specific to the first two rounds of the playoffs?

Another potential limitation relates to the choice of the newspaper *La Presse*. It is possible that the articles selected conveyed only a francophone perspective and that the perspective of anglophones was excluded as a consequence.

With respect to the articles themselves, it should be noted that they were written by three or four hockey reporters. Aren't the characteristics identified a reflection of their nostalgia or their biases? Perhaps. But note that the articles include many excerpts from interviews with players and therefore do not flow strictly from the pen (and the opinion) of the journalist (even though the excerpts included are also a matter of journalistic choice), who in any case is not immune from social influences.

The objection could also be made that the discourses of the players (and of the journalists) in our work are very formulaic and that redundancy is to be expected. We do not deny this. Nevertheless, these formulas in no way block the expression of social normativity; what is difficult to decipher in social norms is precisely those formulaic, commonsense discourses that are sometimes so internalized that they appear to be "natural."

Finally, our analysis of social normativity should also be viewed from a temporal perspective. Did the characteristics attributed to players in the 1950s reflect the social norms prevalent during that period? Are normative changes visible through the prism of hockey? Further longitudinal studies on this point would be useful and enlightening.

From Normative Gap to Pathology

By way of conclusion, we would like to go back to the past, more precisely to February 2009, when Alexei Kovalev, the former number 27 of Le Grand Club, was forced to take time off. General manager Bob Gainey had been quite direct at the time: "The team doesn't need Kovalev the way he's playing currently." In other words (and this was not specific to Alex Kovalev's case), a player was benched when his profitability and productivity (here the number of goals per game) did not meet the organization's requirements. What is very interesting here is not Kovalev's lack of fitness, but rather the interpretation that was made of this departure from the standard of performance.

In fact, this impossibility of meeting the demands of the Canadiens fans and of the team owners was interpreted from the perspective of a pathology. "I don't have ten examples to give you, but this kind of thing has already been seen," coach Guy Carbonneau said at a press conference. "Athletes are not immune. In the business world, we see people take months off because of a depression."

Here, the departure from the performance requirement was "pathologized." The analogy with the social world is very rich, since we find here the fundamental social question of the boundary between a normal phenomenon and a pathological one. These days, the distinction between a "depressed" person and a "non-depressed" person is difficult to establish and can sometimes simply depend on the number of days of insomnia or hypersomnia, a state of sadness, or the like. It is even mentioned explicitly in the *DSM-IV-TR* (the reference manual for mental disorders) that the number of people who have a disorder is an objective criterion for defining a mental illness. Without claiming that contemporary psychiatry has rigorously reduced the phenomenon of depression to a statistical deviation, it tells us that the parameters of the normal and the pathological are not very clear today. This absence of a precise boundary between a "non-depressed" and a "depressed" individual can also be related to the failure to take into account the etiological factors of the phenomenon of depression or the reduction of this mental disorder to a visible set of signs and symptoms: "I saw in his eyes that he needs a little rest," said Bob Gainey.

So it is hardly surprising that the possible depression of a hockey player is calculated in terms of the number of games played without scoring goals. The athlete's statistics are, in a way, our insomnia. We can "miss" a few nights, but after a few weeks, consultations, and even medication, are required. Here then is a first stigmatization: interpreting a departure from social norms as pathology. This process is called the *medicalization of social issues*.

And to continue with our reasoning, if Alex Kovalev had really been depressed, what should have been done? How could he have been helped? The response of the Montreal Canadiens was to bench him for a while. This method seems to stigmatize a player, since today we ask individuals to support those suffering from mental problems and certainly not to exclude them. The second phase of Kovalev's stigmatization thus involved taking charge of him – managing his problem, one might say.

Of course, the Kovalev case is more complex than what we have just described. In addition, how the professional sports club took charge of him includes parameters for which we have not accounted. We would highlight here that in our society, as in the area of sports, a departure from current social norms (and especially performance) is too often interpreted in the language of pathology. This is dangerous for the individual but also for the society, since one usually recognizes the "greatness" of a society by the way it treats its marginal citizens.

Moreover, the departure from the standard – from the potential "deviance" – is sometimes seen as a way to rethink the modalities of intervention, to borrow from the vocabulary of social workers. In this case, had Kovalev been heard from? What did his poor performances say about the club and its management? Wasn't there a way to include him in rethinking the organization of the lines? Was it a problem of the players or of the team? In short, once again, the marginal was condemned to silence ...

The Montreal Canadiens are at the heart Quebecers' debates and discussions. The fact that they occupy so much space in the media (one or two hours a day even when there are no games) is a reflection on ourselves, not by proxy but normatively.

NOTES

1 In this way, the fans' sense of belonging to Le Grand Club is similar to that of certain European soccer clubs where the team, the city, and local industries inextricably linked and are key to the social bond (Bromberger, 1995).
2 All of the characteristics mentioned will be analysed except for the physical involvement, which, because it remains specific to athletic contests, is difficult to extrapolate to society.

4 The Montreal Canadiens as a Popular Object: Representations of Tradition

FANNIE VALOIS-NADEAU

What are the Montreal Canadiens? A team, a business, an object of worship, an object of memory, or a heritage? Perhaps a little of everything at once. The Canadiens (and even more broadly, hockey) are often labelled "national" or even "religious," because the team occupies an important place in Quebec life, whether by filling the media with comments and analyses, structuring agendas, or being an object of cultural reference. How are we then to reflect on this particular, plural, and varied subject? How are we to grasp it in its multiplicity and do justice to its complexity? How at the same time are we to bear witness to its singularity as a professional sports team that has taken part in the cultural and political life of Quebec for more than a century? I have given up trying to locate the essence and intrinsic value of the Canadiens except by studying the qualities attributed to them by various actors.

Given the enthusiasm in the media and in the business world for the Montreal Canadiens in recent years, I examined the representations that constitute this popular object.[1] Through an analysis of the discussion forums hosted by the website the Réseau des sports (RDS) and posted during the seasons 2006–7 and 2007–8, I observed the representations constructed by the team's fans through their many exchanges. Having set out to answer the impossible question "What do the Montreal Canadiens represent?," I found myself instead observing "how the Montreal Canadiens are represented." This nuance makes all the difference: instead of dwelling on the supposed intrinsic value of the team, we direct our gaze towards the always shifting practices and images that constitute the representations. In this analysis, one dominant narrative through which the Canadiens have been formed relates to "tradition."

The Canadiens are often apprehended with respect to another period; in this way, they have become a cultural object through which relations to time, the self, the community, and space (among other things) are created. When we analyse this discursive process, we find it impossible to see this sports spectacle as an activity that implies the passivity of viewers. On the contrary, what emerges is the creation of a relationship with the world and of ways of discussing society.

The analysis of hockey in Canadian society in recent years has been marked above all by a political economy approach, one that criticizes the sport's increasing commercialization, spectacularization, and internationalization.[2] These texts nevertheless highlight how fans work to make hockey an object of identity. Avoiding a focus on the actions and advertising campaigns of the team owners (while recognizing the importance of these in the representation process), this analysis examines instead the discourse of the fans in and through which are constructed emotional relations and questions of power. To understand how francophone fans represent the team, I will situate my research as part of cultural studies; this will make it possible to consider the Canadiens as the product of a specific situational articulation. It is this articulation that interests me, for it has generated a phenomenon that is specific to Quebec.

To this end, it seems first of all necessary to discuss how I see the Canadiens in all their multiplicity and in all the spaces they occupy. Associated with daily life, with leisure, with heritage, with tradition, but also with spectacle, commerce, and industry, the Canadiens are a good example of the concept of popular culture, wherein "economics" and "culture" cannot be separated (Du Gay, 1997). Then, by emphasizing the sports media complex, I will examine how the spectacle of the Canadiens gives these representations reality by being both cultural activity and commentary. After that, I will present two dimensions that have emerged in posts collected on the RDS discussion forums: in one, various concepts of the foreign player have been condensed; in the other, the commodification of hockey is fiercely debated.

An analysis of discussion forums related to the Canadiens permits an interpretation of the tensions that run through and constitute contemporary popular culture. The premise for this reflection is the idea that popular culture is neither good nor bad (nor should it be seen as such); it is simply (albeit in a very complex way) a field in which is articulated, in a more or less hegemonic and conflictual way, a multitude of representations (Hall, 2005).

The Montreal Canadiens: A Complex Object of Popular Culture

Examining the Montreal Canadiens as a cultural phenomenon necessarily involves thinking about ways to understand popular culture. The approach used throughout this analysis is based on that of cultural studies, which has positioned itself at the crossroads of theories about cultural industries, social anthropology, and working-class history. Cultural studies, which focuses on the popular, is not a very dogmatic field and cannot be summarized in a few lines. Nevertheless, I have selected a few contributions to that current as starting paradigms.

The first aspect of popular culture analyses relates to their conceptualization – they are almost always accompanied by value judgments. Whether celebrated or held in contempt, whether viewed as authentic (the culture of the "real" people) or as a pure fabrication, popular culture is often constructed through another figure (Storey, 2001) – that is, in opposition to elite culture, to art, tradition, or folklore, to the bourgeoisie, or the like. However, given that the Canadiens participate both in an established tradition and in cultural industries, and given that they are consumed (albeit in various ways) by people in all walks of life, this dichotomy does not hold for the team. Instead of conceptualizing popular culture through its supposed shortcomings, I will be emphasizing all of those interconnections that have made the Canadiens a specific cultural object. In other words, I understand the Habs to be a point of convergence for many cultural components and not as some sort of underbelly of a national or artistic culture.

The second point taken from this theoretical current, which is of considerable importance in the analysis I will be carrying out, is that I recognize the capacity for action and protest through cultural practices, whatever the socio-economic status of the individuals. As Stuart Hall has pointed out, it is possible to negotiate and resist cultural hegemony even while being part of it (Hall, 1997, pp. 24–26, 42–51). Instead of understanding the enthusiasm for the Canadiens in terms of manipulation and alienation, as followers of the Frankfurt School would, my emphasis will be on the potential "agency" of the actors.[3] The constitution of meaning is a situational process that is far from automatic and unidirectional. It is also much more complex than the linear communication chain of transmitter–receiver,

To avoid these pitfalls, my entry point to understanding the complexity and indeed the very existence of the Canadiens as a Quebec cultural phenomenon is precisely the articulation of the representations that bring it to life. I mean by articulation

> the form of the connection that can make a unity of two different elements, under certain conditions. It is a linkage which is not necessary, determined, absolute and essential for all time. You have to ask, under what circumstances can a connection be forged or made? The so-called "unity" of a discourse is really the articulation of different, distinct elements which can be rearticulated in different ways because they have no necessary "belongingness." The "unity" which matters is a linkage between the articulated discourse and the social forces with which it can, under certain historical conditions, but need not necessarily, be connected. (Stuart Hall, quoted in Slack, 1996)

This means, for example, questioning how representations of the Canadiens articulate salient issues in present-day Quebec. These articulations – which here will be structured around tradition, ethnicity, and commodification, without being their sole, definitive, constitutive threads – can be broken down and reconstituted differently, depending on the successes (and failures) of the team. Across all the articulations presented, one observation remains when we think about the uniqueness of the Canadiens: the importance of the French language.

Besides making the team the historical emblem of a city and of many communities, representations of the Canadiens permit the promotion of the variety of interests and ways of thinking. In producing discourses related to the team, the actors – each in their own way – create various meanings and images over time. Sometimes these are contradictory, sometimes complementary. For example, the Canadiens were, successively, the standard bearers of the French Canadians (with the Flying Frenchmen) as well as the bilingual emblem of the City of Montreal (with the famous Punch Line). It is possible to view today's team as an object of heritage, memory, and worship. So I do not want to attribute an essence to the Canadiens; quite the contrary, I want to show how they have evolved over time, according to the aspirations of the actors and the circumstances of the moment. Although my analysis focuses on the meaning the fans give their team, when we consider the phenomenon as a whole, we cannot reduce it to the actions of a single type of actor. These actors do not operate in a vacuum – on the contrary, their productions are constantly intermingling.

This means we must observe *how people make meaning* from their world, especially through discourse. It is a matter not of conducting a semiological analysis of the texts offered by the fans, but rather of looking at which texts these fans use to express their attachment to the Canadiens. For most of the authors of the texts studied, the team has been associated with a collective history and quotidian life since childhood.[4] Because fans count on the Canadiens to defend and honour Montreal, Quebec, or Canadian culture, their relationship to the team is often passionate. The views of the Canadiens posted on discussion forums are often highly emotional. For Lawrence Grossberg, who has examined the place of affect in the practices of popular culture, affect does not simply emanate from the reading of a text – it is (especially) a particular way of doing things that gives meaning to a practice. Such "affective alliances," as he calls them, have their own "logic and coherence (though these are often very difficult to define), depending upon their affective relationships, their articulated places within people's mattering maps" (Grossberg, 1992, p. 80). As we will see, representations of the Canadiens are closely connected to a collective identity – be it a Montreal, Quebec, or pan-Canadian identity – which is very often constituted by a linguistic dimension (though not solely by that dimension).

Since the Canadiens constitute for their fans a form of belonging, the combinations of representations are not insignificant – quite the contrary. I will be analysing the coherence produced in these representations, as well as how those representations are disseminated, in order to see which ones are emphasized more than others. The content on the online forums may depart greatly from the historical facts presented in certain books; what is pertinent, for me, is the work of reorganization undertaken by those who participate in those forums. As we analyse the discussion forums, we will observe that the Canadiens are not a homogeneous symbol that conveys the stories and traditions of a people; rather, they are a cultural entity in which are shaped many representations of the team – and the cultures that invest it.

Spectator Sport as Effectivity of Collective Belonging

Spectator sport is a very rich object of investigation, for it can be understood as a particular cultural formation, one that is related to all kinds of issues (gender, social class, ethnicity, etc.). Spectator sport is not something to be deplored, nor is it a phenomenon that distracts us from "real" civic debates; rather, it is a site where certain civic and political debates are constituted and defined. The sites of these debates are not limited to the traditional Habermasian public sphere; they can be expanded into other spaces, thus avoiding compartmentalizing the political aspects of daily life. Spectator sports do not reflect the society that pre-exists them; they are a full-fledged cultural activity, an integral part of society.

Various discourses and representations, then, are produced and actualized through spectator sport. In "Come Together: Sport, Nationalism, and the Media Image," David Rowe, Jim McKay, and Toby Miller pointed out the effectivity of representations of the nation through such spectacles:

> The nation is conjured up at those moments when an affective unity can be posited against the grain of structural divisions and bureaucratic taxonomies. This is the cultural nation we experience through diverse feelings, policies, and practices, the parameters of which are inherently difficult to define. (2000, p. 120)

From the *experience* of opposition to a rival group (and from all the sensations and emotions that can result from this) arise representations of a collective whole, which are closely linked to cultural and territorial forms of organization (municipal, regional, national, ethnic, etc.).

Referring to the writings of Benedict Anderson, Rowe and his colleagues point out that it is impossible to fully grasp the materiality and the overarching character of even the smallest nations. That is why the nation becomes manifest and effective in the imaginary of the people through representative artefacts – hence Benedict Anderson's "imagined entity" and "perceptual horizon." Through representation, the nation is materialized and made concrete and disseminated. From this perspective, spectator sports are one form of representation through which the community becomes tangible. Hockey and the Canadiens are among the artefacts that constitute the perceptual horizon in Canada and Quebec. Represented as part of the history of a country and a people and watched by large numbers of the inhabitants, the Habs are a cultural activity and spectacle through which various elements of identity are formed. But unlike other Canadian teams, it constitutes for many Quebec fans a nation articulated around linguistic issues.

One sphere associated with spectator sports that participates in this effectivity, thanks to the daily visibility it allows, is the media sphere. Hockey – here, the Canadiens – has been stimulating discussion from the start, for more than a century. The Canadiens are the subject of newspaper articles, but they are also part of everyday texts, that is, conversations in public places, in the workplace, in families, in games, in leisure activities, and so on. Talking about the Canadiens, whether in discussion forums or during lunch at work, is an activity that leads to encounters, converging interests, even a certain cohesiveness. Independently of opinions on the performance of the team, the important thing seems to be that this talk is a daily activity shared by many. As mentioned by Gruneau and Whitson in *Hockey Night in Canada*, hockey has become one of the most powerful Canadian symbols by being part of the Canadian way of life – by being both the myth and the allegory of that culture. Hockey makes it possible for us to recount to one another daily who we are. I would add that the very activity of recounting ourselves to one another daily is what *makes* us who we are.

Analysis of Representations of the Montreal Canadiens

Discussions about the Montreal Canadiens are greatly influenced by the athletic performance of the club. For example, over the 2007–8 season,[5] during which the interventions were collected, the general climate of the discussions varied greatly and one player could go from "hero to zero" very quickly (Kovalev's case is especially eloquent). The concepts of "foreigner" and "merchandise" were recurrent in conversations about the team. Rather than exhaustively reviewing the literature on these subjects, I will be pointing to their resonance in the RDS discussion forums and describing the polarization of discussions. Avoiding the easy diagnosis of "Quebecers who no longer recognize themselves and who have lost their reference points," the following analysis will focus on the creation and negotiation of representations associated with these dimensions.

The Figure of the Foreigner: Between Integration and Rejection

Across the discussion forums, two positions emerged on the subject of a multiethnic team. Both were based on performance rather than on the direct representation of the citizenry. One related to the rejection and criticism of the current model, the other to integration of the foreigner. In these two diametrically opposed perceptions, "good player" representations combined constantly with identity representations. In a context in which concepts of nationality and language were amalgamated to represent "the real player from here," and in which politicians demanded a French-speaking team captain,[6] representations of the Montreal Canadiens were mixed up with those of Quebecers.

First of all, it is interesting that how the contributors *define* a foreign player is mainly a function of how they characterize the collectivity to which they feel they belong (francophone, Quebecer, Canadian, hockey fans, etc.). This is followed by a hierarchy of these characteristics, one that fluctuates enormously among the contributors.[7] In general, Europeans – especially Russians – are criticized for not taking to heart the defence of the Canadiens' honour – and that of the public that supports them. The appeal to tradition – a return to "origins" – is an organizing principle of this discourse. By that very fact, it constitutes an interplay of boundaries between the self and the other.[8]

In this type of argument, representations of the Montreal Canadiens as an originally Quebec and francophone team are frequently encountered. Around this representation, an obvious and natural link is made between the team's success and its francophone composition.[9] Ethnicity thus becomes an indicator of success, and the representation of a team with a diverse past, in terms of both national identity and linguistic identity, becomes a prominent factor. Bilingualism as a constitutive dimension of the team since the end of the Maroons, the Punch Line (an illustrious trio made up of francophone and anglophone players), and local anglophone stars like Howie Morenz (remember that thousands came to his funeral in the Forum to pay their final respects) are not taken into account in that essentialist discourse. The fact that the members of the Flying Frenchmen (who are used to explain success in terms of ethnicity) came from outside Quebec makes all the more striking the combination of the concepts of ethnicity, culture, nation, and language in the constitution of the image of "Quebec" and "foreign" players.

Marked by an ethnic nationalism, this discourse folds together certain attributes that are supposedly valued in Quebec by attaching them to Quebec players. For example, heart (courage, commitment, honour, etc.) and perseverance, especially as exemplified by the Quebec players Francis Bouillon and Steve Bégin, become through these discourses specifically Québécois characteristics. For many forum participants, this devotion, which seems almost an intrinsic characteristic of a nationality, is apparently valued more than the talent and skills of a Kovalev.

When the team is struggling, a return to the good old days is envisaged, with the "foreign" elements eliminated:

> The problem with the Montreal Canadiens is that they have nine Europeans in the lineup. That's too many. We saw the result yesterday: they played like little girls. It was pathetic. The Europeans on our team don't want to deliver because they don't want to get injured so that they're healthy for the world championship in May. That is why ... I want North American players and not European players who take it easy in the playoffs. I want Quebecers, like in 1993. (hadi04, 2008/04/20; translation)

Because they will be representing their country after the playoffs, the European players are suspected of assigning more importance to their nation than to the Habs. Denouncing their lack of devotion and determination, these forum participants depict the foreign players (and especially the Russians) as players without passion or emotion. "Heart" and "balls"[10] are the prerogative of American and, especially, Canadian players. Virility and Canadianness thus become complementary. It is interesting that in the presence of the figure of the foreigner, Quebecers, Canadians, and North Americans are blended together in these representations.

With regard to opponents, representations of the "foreigner" are not as problematic. Particularly interesting here is that the various discursive elements are still consistent with a narrative of tradition, but one that is interpreted in a very different way. When asked if they thought that the foreign players were proud to be playing for the Canadiens, many contributors compared the development of those players with that of the team's fans. The culture connected to the sport is considered to be the same if its players have shared the same hostile winter environment (which according to many forum participants, is not that of the southern United States, where there are several NHL teams). Skating outside in winter contributes to an image of hockey that is *experienced*, that is part of the culture.

The sharing of a childhood spent admiring hockey stars also serves this same narrative. So that everyone speaks the same language, the language of hockey, the childhood heroes are the same (or at least, they are all hockey players) and are put on the same level as the elite of the sport. In the same way, major events related to the sport that have contributed to establishing it as a tradition, such as the Canadiens–Red Army match-up, are represented as common benchmarks for everyone who is passionate about hockey, whether they are players or fans: "The Kostitsyns [from Belarus] said that they were proud of playing for the team that played against the Red Army team, that they watched videos of the 31 December game when they were kids" (shadowhunter, 10 March 2008; translation).

Finally, many forum participants talked about the pride the players could feel in playing for the Canadiens, a century-old organization with more championships than any other hockey team. Aware of the history associated with the team, the players of different origins would therefore be united in carrying on the glorious history of the team, represented as being as important as any other sports dynasty:

> I believe very seriously [that they are proud of it]. Especially Kovalev ... When Kovalev signed here, he said that he wanted to be part of the history of the Canadiens ... Subsequently, after a spectacular performance against the Rangers, Kovalev said that he was proud to have written a piece of the history of the Canadiens. (olipower, 10 March 2008; translation)

When placed on the same footing as the major European football clubs, the Canadiens are an institution that imposes recognition and pride. By uniting a single childhood with a single dream and a single history, these contributors fashion the team's foreign players in a way that renders them both familiar and similar to the self. Although the differences are still pronounced, this implementation of the tradition comes close to representations of the "self" and of the "foreigner."

The team's ethnic make-up is a hot topic in the various forums. Some discussions of the Canadiens implicitly include this discourse on who are (or should be) Quebecers. The discussions on foreign players and Quebecers in this way integrate xenophobic discourses with discourses on tolerance in Quebec's public space. But always, the hockey players are viewed above all according to their nationalities and their ability to express themselves in French, making those dimensions very significant in the reading of hockey.

The Commercialization of the Team: Between Criticisms and Appropriation Mechanisms

The second focus of this narrative of tradition is related to the commercialization of the Montreal Canadiens. Again, there are two opposing positions, each contributing in its way to reaffirming the status of tradition associated with the Canadiens. On the one hand, large-scale commercialization of the club is criticized, in particular because it is distant from the sports practices of the past, which are considered more authentic. On the other, identification with the team, which has been made into a tradition, is carried out directly through the consumption of merchandise. The Montreal Canadiens in this way have become an object of enduring worship. This opposition is interesting because it gives shape to a tradition comprised solely of "cultural" elements as well as to commercialization carried out solely in the "economic" sphere, as if both fields were recent, with the existence of one erased in favour of the other. Basing my work on a popular culture approach in which "economy" and "culture" can be thought of independently of each other, I focus in this section on analysing that relationship, which is ambiguous at best. Again, in this type of discussion, in which the forum participants show what they want to belong to, it is possible to recognize the critical potential of fans. Beyond a reading defined simply in terms of resistance or hegemony, all kinds of representations of social changes are combined.

The representation of the Canadiens (i.e., as a Quebec cultural object) competes with that of the NHL, which focuses more on economic profitability than on the maintenance of the sport in its original form.[11] Many fans are not happy about this, especially when the visibility of Quebec and Canada is diminished, and when the league expands into "unnatural" markets by moving teams and so on. The commercialization of hockey and the NHL very often becomes a synonym for Americanization. Various hockey personalities, such as the former Canadiens owner George Gillett and NHL commissioner Gary Bettman, represent this "Americanization" and are viewed as responsible for changes to "local" traditions. In appeals for respect for the world before the Bettmans and Gilletts,[12] the forum participants construct a discourse on the required representativity of the collectivity:

> In fact, I believe that it is rather a question of respect. Any company doing business in another country or receiving foreign capital has to know and respect the culture of its customers or its investors. The Montreal Canadiens is a business that makes money from Quebec customers of which the vast majority are Francophone. Therefore, I believe honestly that the representative should ... establish a respectful connection that units the two clans. And I repeat, it is a matter of respect. (patatepilee, 16 October 2007; translation)

By denouncing the lack of "respect" on the part of the corporate sector, this forum participant is producing an image of the collectivity and the traditions to be respected. The vast majority of discussions in this vein express a romantic vision of old-time hockey, the game as played on ponds, in alleys, and in parks. This representation of yesteryear hockey is realized through a relationship with purity, authenticity – through the beauty of the game and true competition (based on defence of the honour of the place) and the heart the players used to put into earning their stripes, before all this was tainted by money. It is interesting that this type of representation completely ignores the importance of urbanization in the development of the spectator sport, as well as the presence of the media, which has always provided it with daily coverage. Hockey as we know it today developed in a show business system; capital and marketing were required for the sport's visibility, which led to its current status as a tradition (see also Bélanger and Valois-Nadeau, 2009). Without denying the constraints of the economic system in which hockey developed, the fact remains that it is in its show-business dimension that hockey (and the Canadiens) has acquired its fame.

Yet representations of the looming Americanization of hockey define commodification as an element exterior to the sport – not as part of a tradition but rather as an indication of the decline in a certain way of doing things. Once again, we find here traces of a discourse on ethnicity: this form of commercialization is seen as external to practices that are specific to Quebec.

In a very different way, the comments collected from discussion forums suggest that Canadiens fans have often internalized this commercialization logic, in particular through heavy consumption of symbols of the Canadiens. Commercialization of the Canadiens becomes a way for fans to express their sense of belonging and to embrace the team tradition, whether by wearing the club logo or decorating their basements with the team colours or memorabilia:

> No choice but to confess, concerning the "CH tattooed on the heart," that famous tattoo that I really have, but on the arm. My basement at home is a little museum of the CH. I had seen advertising from Home Depot that featured the colours of the NHL, and well last year I completely redid my basement in its entirety in the colours of the Canadiens, decorated with all kinds of collector's items from the Habs. Moreover, the centrepiece of my collection, which I love the most, is an Aurèle Joliat

> hockey card, not very new that one! Let's say that it's pretty easy to get into the mood with my friends on game nights! Goodtime-Charlie, you say bravo; others will say instead that it's too much, but it doesn't matter, it makes me happy. In the evening, when I go home, there isn't one day goes by that I don't go down to my basement saying to myself, I feel good here, I'm happy ... it's the basement of my dreams! (Stanley Cup, 7 March 2007; translation).

Many objects are kept for the purpose of venerating them and keeping alive the memories with which they are associated: "I also have Coke and Molson 1993 cans and the 1993 cap. I have the original 45 record of the song *Bleu blanc rouge*" (the human machine, 7 April 2008; translation). Of course, the contributors do not all have the same relationship with the team and the same need to materialize it, but generally we can recognize in forums the happiness and pride those objects provide. This way of showing your sense of belonging to the team through merchandise makes it possible to situate the importance of objects for the process of identification. Making allegiances visible helps reaffirm the link between fans and the team, but also the links among fans. The objects that represent the Canadiens tradition are one way through which fans establish their loyalty.

This commercialization process is an important means of transmitting the tradition of the team (and, indeed, of creating that tradition), and the Canadiens organization capitalizes on this. But the fans, too, participate in everything that is represented as tradition, by investing certain objects with that tradition rather than others. In the end, whether through commercialized products or through caustic criticism of the sport's commodification, always created is a sense of belonging through the diverse representations of the sport, the collectivity, customs, and so on.

The Common Thread of Tradition

Analysing the exchanges of the forum participants in terms of representations makes it possible to understand what comprises the Montreal Canadiens. From this perspective, the Canadiens are not conveying meanings that must be revealed; rather, they are a cultural object through which certain forms of identity materialize, certain concepts of tradition, of Quebecness, and so on. An important point made in this analysis relates to the fluctuation and dynamism of representations of the "foreigner" and "us," currently and in the past. In light of what has been presented here, it is impossible to see the fans as a homogeneous whole or the Montreal Canadiens as a cultural object with *one* true value. This, however, does not prevent me from observing that tradition, as the framework structuring discussions, is constantly being applied. The representations that have been mentioned feature a certain concept of "another" period, on the basis of which take shape many relationships of belonging.

In discussions about foreign players and the commercialization of the team, tradition is brought up in two distinct ways. On the one hand, it helps underscore changes (even clear breaks) from one period to the next, which are explained by the presence of elements considered "external." Here, tradition is represented as a form of authenticity to be preserved. By claiming to be resisting the current dominant order, these forum participants create, at various levels, hegemonic representations of unity and authenticity that exclude any foreign element. But at the same time, tradition is evoked to point out common bases that are permeable to time and to geographic boundaries. The sense of belonging to the team is thus achieved through a certain representation of its sporting heritage, without it being linked to a concept of ethnicity and the collectivity. The community of fans thus takes precedence over the civic, ethnic, or linguistic community. However, these representations base the team's value on a certain past. Each in its own way, these two representations of tradition show a certain conservatism, a desire to *preserve*.

The representations of the Canadiens are therefore paradoxical. The Habs are criticized for being overly commercial but at the same time are associated with a great unifying popular tradition. They are the symbol both of the commercialization of Quebec culture and of what is consolidated by that sense of belonging. The Canadiens are in this way represented by the combination of the local and the international, of heritage and consumer product. In the same way, the Habs articulate various issues, which compete with one another. These articulations are not always clear or coherent. At times, according to the contributors, the Habs are a *Canadian* team, especially when the sport's origins are discussed. But at other times, the linguistic dimension becomes the one to be defended and no longer seems connected to Canadianness. The representations of the Canadiens are always being recombined, rearticulated. Currently (in February 2013) the fact that the team has a general manager and a coach of francophone origins, and its recent surprising successes, have made fans forget criticisms that the captain is a unilingual anglophone. Complaints sometimes arise about the small number of francophone players on the team, but these are never shared by all the fans or among all media. There is one constant: the image of the Canadiens is always created on the basis of varied discourses that create multiple forms of belonging. The Canadiens are far from being simply a form of escapism that permits the masses to let off steam. On the contrary, this hockey club permits the materialization of belonging, which is certainly not unidimensional.

NOTES

1 The conclusions I present here are based on my master's thesis in sociology (UQAM, 2009).
2 The writings by Richard Gruneau and David Whitson have had great resonance in Canadian literature on hockey. See, for example, Gruneau and Whitson (1993).
3 This approach is not intended to supplant the power relations present in the very constitution of these representations, but rather to apprehend it in terms of hegemony, in which the concepts of negotiation and resistance make it possible to see *something else*.
4 Although anonymous, most of the interlocutors in my sample seemed to me to have been born in Quebec or, if not, to have lived there for quite a long time in order to share with others their memories of the team.
5 While the conclusions of the analysis presented are based on comments on the 2007–2008 season, it would still be possible today to find traces during the subsequent seasons. We would just have to think of the controversies following the hiring of Randy Cunneyworth (a unilingual anglophone) as head coach.
6 Remember in this regard the scandal caused by Guy Bertrand and Pauline Marois when they made such a demand in 2007. The recent debate around the construction of the amphitheatre in Quebec City, proposed by the Parti Québécois, could be part of the same political aim.
7 In general, a player from the United States is seen as less foreign than one from Belarus. The geographic distance seems to be responsible for the "cultural" distance, except perhaps in cases of francophone players from France or Switzerland.
8 Ironically, it was the Detroit Red Wings, a team made up largely of European players, that won the Stanley Cup in the season when these

comments were made. Their captain, from Sweden, was the first European captain to win this honour.

9 For further information on the percentage of francophone players on the Canadiens, from its founding to the 1960s, see Black (1997).

10 In addition to attributing attributes of perseverance and determination to Quebec players in order to show how they are different from the so-called foreign players, attributes of masculinity are also used to promote Quebec players. The characteristics associated with what is foreign or female are immediately devalued. They are used to indicate what is considered to be bad or meagre.

11 The National Hockey League comprises 30 professional hockey clubs, including the Montreal Canadiens. Originally made up of six clubs (one of which was the Canadiens), the league has expanded its market by establishing teams in places where hockey was a sport that was neither practised nor watched.

12 Since 2009, the team again became the property of the Molson family, which is of Montreal origin and played a decisive role in the history of the Montreal Canadiens starting in the sixties, in particular with the move to the Bell Centre in 1996 and with the creation of a synergistic relationship between the sports and brewing industries (Bélanger, 2000).

5 Is Culture a Factor Here? The Implications of the Corporation of the Montreal Canadiens for Quebec Society

AUDREY LAURIN-LAMOTHE

The popularity enjoyed by the Canadiens is no reason to refrain from criticizing them. By establishing various franchises in the southern United States, the NHL showed that professional hockey is today broadly foreign to its traditional roots and to local popular culture (Whitson and Gruneau, 2006, p. 22). The means the league uses to launch franchises in these communities by speeding up the establishment of the identity of a club with its new city suggest that a systematic analysis of the link between culture and corporation is relevant. Think of Anaheim, which is in a way the perfect example of an expansion strategy: after the popular success of its film *The Mighty Ducks*, the Walt Disney Company asked for and obtained a franchise from the NHL. Its home city became Anaheim, a suburb of Los Angeles, and extensive marketing campaigns were organized there.

This chapter examines the growing presence of the Montreal Canadiens in our society, as a corporation, first of all, and then as a corporation woven into the social fabric. The first part of this chapter describes the decisive moments in the organization's corporate development, moments that will bring to light the dominant characteristics of this type of business. The second part analyses the role of the organization in the society and its involvement in both popular and mass culture.

The Birth of the Canadiens and Its Public, or, How to Build a Tradition

It is well known that in its beginnings, in 1909, the club was comprised almost exclusively of French Canadian players. What is perhaps less known is that the market for high-level hockey then became divided along ethnic, linguistic, and religious lines. The Canadiens were the new team of businessman John Ambrose O'Brien, of the National Hockey Association (NHA), who wanted to surpass a French Canadian team that already existed but that belonged to a rival league – Le National of the Canadian Hockey Association (CHA).

O'Brien was fighting for a prominent place in the sport, and the Canadiens were the tool that would enable his to drain Le National of its vital forces. Didier Pitre and "Newsy" Lalonde were two well-known players who traded in their National jerseys for Habs sweaters (Black, 1997, pp. 26–27). O'Brien waved his money under the nose of a league that at the time was facing financial ruin. That was all it took for the CHA to concede defeat and merge with its rival. The Canadiens then became the only team representing French Canadians.

This was not simply a transfer of property. No more would the National be a means to democratize and disseminate hockey among francophones, through the CHA; the Canadiens of the NHA would be a commercial team whose primary purpose would be to generate profits. At this point, sports and leisure had yet to become integral to daily life for the middle class – both were still reserved for Montreal's anglophone elite.

The amateur association that had founded Le National had grown out of efforts at grassroots education and a desire to carve out a place where French Canadians could socialize (Harvey, 2006, p. 33). So what Montrealers also lost when Le National folded was the educational dimension of sport, which now gave way to strict financial profitability.

But it was not a complete win for O'Brien. By imposing his league and his team, he drew the fire of many fans of Le National, who thought they could smell in the new team money from the west end of the city. For O'Brien, the NHA was a bobble, a pastime, compared to his Ontario mines.

Passion for hockey very quickly became connected to the pursuit of profit. Soon after the Habs were founded, the notion that they were more virtuous, or a fount of French Canadian identity, was widely accepted. Almost all of the players on the earliest Canadiens teams were French Canadian, and this strengthened the fans' attachment. For the Habs owners, this meant higher profits from playing their team against other Montreal teams. When the Maroons, a club from the city's west end and the Habs' principal rival, declared bankruptcy in 1938, the Canadiens set out to redefine their image by abandoning their ethnic, religious, and linguistic roots in order to incorporate the now "homeless" Maroons fans, most of whom were anglophones. The Punch Line (1943–8), made up of a French Canadian (Maurice Richard) and two English Canadians (Elmer Lach and Toe Blake) would make a huge contribution to this reconfiguration of identity.

The popularity of the Canadiens grew from season to season in the 1910s and 1920s, but never outside Montreal. Only with the coming of radio (1938) and then television (1952) did the Habs become the team of *all* Quebecers, urban and rural. The mass media, with their power to unite people's territories and aspirations, were of great benefit to organizations like the Canadiens, allowing them to spread their influence beyond their original base.

The Emergence of the Corporation and the Player "Factory"

From the start, the Canadiens were a capitalist managerial organization; so was the NHL as a whole. Such organizations need to be distinguished from owner-managed companies. Managerial corporations, which came into being in the early twentieth century, are owned by large numbers of shareholders but are run by managers.[1] Also, a corporation is a legal "person" independent of the people running it. During the time of the Canadian Athletic Club (1909–17), 20,000 shares at $10 a share were issued, and shareholders enjoyed privileged access to tickets for events organized by the club. This steady cash flow gave the organization greater autonomy. In this way, the club was able to ensure its longevity and a lasting presence in the social arena.

In corporation theory, the role of managers is to preserve the organization as it develops, by placing themselves between the workers and the owners as experts and as the possessors of knowledge about the corporation's internal and external workings. The Canadiens and the NHL meet these criteria insofar as both attempt to control their own various elements – the players first and foremost, whose performance they must improve and whose behaviour they must control (on this subject, Wong's book [2005] serves as a reference). Unlike a corporation, an owner-managed company cannot control the elements external to it, including the market, an institution in which the company is only one actor. In the era when this type of capitalism was dominant (prior to the twentieth century), there was greater turnover of employees in factories and workers had more control over their activities, as Rolande Pinard has pointed out:

> When the worker bargains the price of his labour, he applies his economic sense of merchandise, which is expressed through institutions of property and contract; these institutions allow the worker to demonstrate his subjectivity, to act as a subject in society: the worker as "owner" of a trade can actually profit from the freedom of the bourgeois market. (Pinard, 2000, pp. 69–70; translation)

Under bourgeois capitalism, this freedom exists only in the market. Once the contract is signed, the labour belongs to capital. Labour, that is, is a commodity subject to economic institutions, but, once it enters the factory, it constitutes only one form of capital in the hands of the capitalist. It follows that by exercising his right to property, the capitalist also exercises the right to manage labour *as* capital, combining it with other forms of capital such as tools and raw materials.

A capitalist who cannot fully exert his right to organize has been deprived of the full enjoyment of his property. On their emergence, corporations would take control of certain economic institutions, such as the labour market, supply and demand, and competition. It is precisely because the Canadiens did not want to suffer from a lack of quality players that they developed those players themselves, thereby controlling the market for them.

To illustrate this organizing tendency: In 1946, Frank Selke, a manager of the Canadiens, established a "system of farm clubs with a team in each province of the country to develop young players and ensure an annual crop" (Bonneau and Hafsi, 1996, p. 54; translation). Unlike other teams, the Canadiens saw the benefits of recruiting young players. By 1952, it had hockey's biggest farm team system, across Canada but also in the United States, with a pool of 1,500 young players. With that network, "the ethnic or linguistic exclusivity the Canadiens benefited from during the 1910–1940 period changed into a 'territorial' exclusivity during the forties and fifties" (Black, 1997, p. 95; translation). The club was able to make this system self-financing by selling players to other NHL teams, which preferred to recruit players from the Canadiens pool rather than develop their own farm teams. It goes without saying that this system put the Canadiens ahead of the game. They were able to keep the best prospects, but also the knowledge of the qualities and weaknesses of the players they sold. This advantage provided by the farm teams, more than any other factor, would contribute to the superiority of the Habs over the following decades.

This system is different from what we have today with, for example, the Hamilton farm team. This old model of farm clubs existed from 1946 to 1967. During those years, boys around ten years of age were selected to be instilled with the values associated with professional hockey. The child, often far from his hometown, was subjected to strict discipline. He became a model employee of the organization:

> The ability of a young player to function according to the values and norms of the club was taken into account as much as his athletic talents. The farm club system was a kind of sieve through which passed only the players who best met the expectations of the managers. Once they had gone through this system, the players were the organization. They were imbued with the organization. They would have played for nothing, just for the pride of putting on that jersey and being in the Forum. (translation)

The authors continue:

> The farm club system is a key element in the improvement of the management of the most important assets of a hockey club, its players. There is no doubt that that it *stimulates* and *organizes* the supply of players. (Bonneau and Hafsi, pp. 119, 65; translation)

Here we see the absorption of the supply (an intrinsic aspect of the market) by the corporation. The Canadiens, by organizing supply and demand, proceeded in the same way as the corporations of the time – that is, the club monopolized the institutions in place and gained the loyalty of the workers.

In the 1950s, the Players' Association fought to be recognized by the NHL. Two of the NHLPA's goals were to improve players' pensions through increased contributions from the clubs and to put an end to exclusive contracts. In its resistance to improving the players' working conditions, the NHL was supported by the US House of Representatives, which exempted four professional sports from the provisions of US antitrust laws. As a result of this protection and consolidation of the market, 96 per cent of NHL players were from sponsored teams by 1996.[2] Subsequent attempts to create rival clubs and leagues further demonstrated the shortage of good players organized by the NHL.

Under that system, the players were confined to an internal market, one in which non-competition clauses prevented them from benefiting from the freedom that the economic institutions of a bourgeois marketplace would have given them. Thus we see that, thanks to the monopoly the league was permitted, the Canadiens were able to ensure for themselves a stable market of players who would comply with the club's expectations. For example, by restricting the mobility of workers on the labour market, corporations hope to stimulate mobility in the *internal* labour market, the one they have created to suit themselves (with provisions for the recognition of seniority, pension plans, insurance, etc.). The famous clause on player mobility was a clear illustration of the exception the sport insisted it should enjoy, in contrast to other capitalist organizations. The pretext being that this restriction offered better entertainment for fans.

Organization under the Coming of Neoliberal Regulation

Towards the end of the 1960s, the farm team system was abandoned (in part because of increasing costs) in favour of a player draft. Also around this time, the NHL expanded in order to maintain hockey's position in the sports market. Since the players were the clubs' most valuable assets, and since recruitment was now carried out mainly through an annual draft, it became crucial for teams to obtain the best draft choices: "The Canadiens changed from being an organization of producers to an organization of prospectors and merchants" (Bonneau and Hafsi, 1996, p. 98; translation).

In a sense, the farm club era was a golden age for hockey organizations – an era when clubs could control their environment, forge lasting links with the players, and substitute the institutional market with an internal market adapted to its needs. The end of the farm clubs the setting up of the universal draft in 1970 can be understood in light of the rise of neoliberal regulation, characterized by an open market and, for the players, increased insecurity.

Pinard's analysis is useful here for understanding these changes. For many years, to control its environment, a hockey organization gained the loyalty of its employees by providing assurances and rewards. It also developed a scientific organization of work (kinesiologists, psychologists, nutritionists, etc.) that among others things entailed creating positions and functions that enabled workers to climb through the ranks (head coach, assistant coach, etc.). These two forces, when combined, increased still more the loyalty of employees to the organization and abolished the external market, the one the club could not control.

Neoliberal regulation would transform this approach to fostering loyalty between employee and employer. The new relationship would be based on flexibility. One might expect the creation of subcontractors and the dismantling of the employee pyramid to bring about greater competition. Far from it. In the dynamics of subcontracting, when there is a true market governed by competition, subcontractors do not make products according to the needs of the head office, but rather according to supply and demand. The corporation of the first half of the twentieth century was a pyramid; a corporation based on neoliberal regulation is a nucleus surrounded by subcontractors, with the connections between the two adjusted according to the principle of flexibility.

In professional hockey, such neoliberal regulation manifested itself in the abandonment of farm clubs and in the creation of a subcorporations that fed the parent corporation. For example, instead of maintaining young players until they were adults for no profit except from a small number of them, the Canadiens benefited from external structures that had been operating prior to the team's involvement. It is interesting to hear broadcasters today on the RDS sports network talk about Quebec players' statistics by referring to the "francophone sector," as if it were a company that should be supported. That sector is comprised of amateur clubs and secondary schools that organize sports studies programs and junior leagues. Thus, without spending a penny, the Canadiens benefit from a high-quality pool of potential players even while generating positive externalities with other organizations. Recall here that the NHL is a monopoly that maximizes its upstream control and the dissemination of the interests of the corporation throughout society. This dissemination of professional hockey throughout society (school, leisure, consumption, television) is the subject of the next section.

From Popular Culture to Mass Culture: The Canadiens in Society

The internal organization of productive elements is inevitably accompanied by an external organization, which is expressed through the team's involvement in institutions of society and mass culture. Without intending to show all the ins and outs of popular culture's links with hockey and the Canadiens, I suggest that the strategies the organization uses have permitted it over the past decade to attract a new generation of fans, despite the team's poor performance.

The real person that was the bourgeois capitalist was gradually replaced by the corporation, which possessed the same rights of property and organization. This new legal "person" was endowed with the same rights as individuals in society. Prior to neoliberal regulation, corporate capitalism then appeared as a moment of transition necessarily oriented towards the corporation's autonomy with respect to individuals. For example, corporate capitalists such as Ford, Nestlé, and Kellogg have gradually freed themselves from the figure of their founder to become brands in themselves. We will see how the Canadiens have followed the same route.

I referred earlier to the educational and recreational structures that support the dissemination of the corporation that is the Canadiens. These structures external to the team never entirely reflect the cultural model imposed on us by the Canadiens. I present here two examples, taken from literature and sociology, that will permit us to understand the variations the Canadiens can contribute in terms of large-scale cultural production, that is, mass culture.

With the Canadiens, the trend towards increasing autonomy with respect to individuals is illustrated among other things by the songs written by the team's fans. Benoît Melançon conducted a historical analysis of their discursive content (Melançon, 2009). He found that the Canadiens, before the 1970s, were referred to largely on the basis of individual players (Richard, Geoffrion, Blake), while in the contemporary period, the emphasis has been more on the team itself. In other words, the songs are less and less about the heroes and more and more about the organization. Although many factors come into play in this phenomenon, there is no question that it reflects a greater dissemination of the brand as such in society and in the collective imaginary. This strengthening of the brand is what permits, for example, the fans to accept the greater mobility of the players.

In the 2009–10 season, one saw in front of the Bell Centre a poster with portraits of Cammalleri, Gionta, Gomez, and Markov that included the inscription "We are Canadiens," as if to help us come to terms with the drastic and ongoing changes in an organization that was now operating under the model of flexibility in order to attain acceptable performance. This tendency was also part of hockey's transition from an institution made up of potentially subversive individuals and heroes (as the Richard/Campbell affair showed), to an organization whose purpose and meaning could be understood through its own dynamic and that purged itself of conflict. If today's fans miss the time of the Canadiens heroes, it is because they see the principle of flexibility and freedom of players as a repudiation of those heroes, and they would not be wrong. Yet we cannot call this commercialization. It seems instead to reflect an Americanization of the sport, in the sense that franchises must be established, in a context of increasing salaries, in bigger and bigger markets, which are located in the United States.

This change in the role of the players is reflected in the writings of Bélanger and Valois-Nadeau, for whom the myth of the Canadiens is sustained by the fans' rejection of its commercialization and by what they see as the perversion of the "real hockey" of yesteryear. Yet, as these authors point out, the hockey of that time was just as commercial as its contemporary version: "The gap between the symbolic history of hockey in Quebec and the material history of the hockey spectacle of the NHL was filled in the last century through a construction that poses hockey as a 'pure' national symbol" (Bélanger and Nadeau, 2009, p. 74; translation).

So it is impossible to separate the myth from the marketing strategies orchestrated by the Canadiens to promote their brand. The move to the Molson Centre (now called the Bell Centre) is an example of the overlapping of brand and myth. A big parade was organized in which the "ghosts" were transported from one arena to another in order to invest the new location with that glorious past. Similar strategies have been adopted by other NHL teams, such as the Maple Leafs, whose marketing division constructed an entire discourse around the idea of carrying the torch from Maple Leaf Gardens to the Air Canada Centre.

How are we to understand the recent marketing strategies of the Canadiens and other NHL clubs? How should we view the Canadiens' new attitude with regard to their promotion, their visibility in the media and in the city, and their relationship with new generations? André Richelieu (2003) shows us that the positioning of sports clubs as brands goes back to the 1990s. Professional teams understood the importance of their history and identity as factors that could be instrumentalized in order to penetrate popular culture and society in general. Promoting yourself as a brand also involves a significant production of merchandise to help create or reinforce a sense of belonging to "the community of the Canadiens." As pointed out by Naomi Klein in her book on brand tyranny, the boundary between cultural event and brand promotion is tending to blur: "It is not to sponsor culture but to *be* culture. And why shouldn't it be? If brands are not products but ideas, attitudes, values and experiences, why can't they be culture too?" (Klein, 2000, p. 30).

Given the dry spell the Habs have gone through since they won their last Stanley Cup in 1993, the managers had to rethink the club's marketing strategy. Not seeing any prospect of taking home that famous trophy in the next few years, Pierre Boivin in 2000 created the position of director of sales and marketing and thoroughly overhauled its approach to both. "Our marketing and sales team has analyzed your needs and your expectations, reinvented our product, segmented our offering, developed a broad range of promotional programs, and redefined the stage management of the evenings to maximize the value of all the time you spend during a game at the Bell Centre" (Boivin, 2004; translation).

A stronger synergy was gradually developed between various partners and the Canadiens. We could mention, among others, the alliance between the corporation and the City of Montreal under the theme "The City Is Hockey" and the distribution of "educational" kits in schools, in addition to standard commercial agreements that multiplied the secondary beneficiaries of the corporation's successes (including the restaurant chain La Cage aux Sports and, since its purchase of the Canadiens, the Molson company).

The creation of the Montreal Canadiens Children's Foundation in 2000 and various other hockey programs aimed at young people propelled the Canadiens as an actor into the domains – to name only these – of violence in hockey and children's health. Founded by Pierre Boivin, Jean Béliveau, and Guy Lafleur, the foundation distributed close to $6 million to 250 organizations (Pronkin, 2009). The foundation and the company are legally independent but are so closely associated that the legal person of the corporation is disguised as a person with ethics. Since the 2000s, the target clientele has become children (in an intergenerational rather than vertical expansion of the consumer base), but also families in general (thus ensuring horizontal expansion, towards women). So despite the absence of Stanley Cup wins, the Canadiens have been able, thanks to finely tuned marketing, to ensure the long-term future of a culture of spectacle and consumption.

To point out how culture and commerce are closely connected is not to deny the symbolic and identity aspects of hockey and the Canadiens. That said, the Canadiens' greatly intensified marketing practices provide food for thought about the types of fans who are answering the call of Le Grand Club. Because, while the Canadiens seem to be gaining in popularity, we need to remember that other clubs have trouble surviving once the novelty of the game wears off. According to Dan Mason, this is what distinguishes *fans* from *flâneurs*: the former are a base of dedicated fans; the latter have a superficial connection to the club, one that is likely to disintegrate at any moment (Mason, 2006).

What Kind of Fan for the Corporation?

In light of this analysis of the corporation, it would be logical to wonder who the typical fan is today. Many political commentators deplore the fact that citizens show little interest in participating in public debate, while TV hockey broadcasts seem to function as true public discussion forums. When the fan backs up his position with statistics on individual or team performances, when he takes part in pools, he is capable of using the best arguments, which, if transposed to the political arena, would make him a model citizen. It is in a way a managerial practice that he is implementing, since everything is done to let him imagine himself in the place of the general manager, managing the millions of dollars and the players – the capital that, when combined, should enrich the corporation. Everything happens as if the passion of the fan were replaced, in our contemporary society, with cold, rational calculation. The sports debate is thus distorted by an accountant's logic, an instrumental rationale.

The figure of the fan has thus been significantly modified since the neoliberal shift, in a dynamics of constant redefinition in relation to what the Canadiens offer. The twentieth-century corporation transformed the market to train workers and gain their loyalty. This relationship changed again during the 1970s to become one characterized by flexibility. At the same time, the corporation has been able to become an integral part of society, and to propose an enduring myth – a symbol. The Canadiens have not been immune to these societal changes, given that hockey as a cultural phenomenon is, and always has been, intrinsically linked to capitalism.

The Canadiens resonate with us because they combine history, national pride, and athletic success. They are able to arouse emotions that consolidate our sense of belonging to them, and all the more so given that they are historically rooted in Quebec society. This syncretism of identity and commerce makes the Canadiens more than a simple company; at the same time, that syncretism strengthens the corporation's capacity to shape our collective identity. Is the corporation exploiting the devotion and unsatisfied fervour of the fans? Is "Forever Yours, the Canadiens" the ultimate means to win the loyalty of the individual?

NOTES

1 Exceptionally, Geoff Molson has been both owner and president of the Canadiens since 2009 – something that has not been seen since 1960.
2 "La LNH à l'abri des lois anti-trusts," *Le Devoir*, 24 February 1966, p. 13. Quoted in Bonneau and Hafsi, 1996, p. 88.

6 "The City Is Hockey": Beyond the Slogan, a Quest for Identity

JONATHAN CHA

Hockey has been for more than a century a mark of Canadian identity. The oldest team in existence, the Montreal Canadiens, celebrated its hundredth anniversary in 2009–10. The festivities for the centenary, which lasted over three seasons, were the most important symbolic event in the City of Montreal since the 350th anniversary of its founding, in 1992. With a view to stimulating "metropolitan" interest, the marketing department of the Canadiens hockey club wanted to raise the Tricolore as the primary "cultural phenomenon" in Montreal by spreading the "good news": hockey is back, and Montreal lives to the rhythm of hockey.

In the post-lockout context, and with all the problems the National Hockey League was going through, in 2006 the Canadiens launched an advertising campaign that directly associated the image of hockey with that of the city. Called "The City Is Hockey," it associated the team with architectural references in Montreal. The city would thus act as a medium for the image of the Habs, and hockey would no longer be just a sport, but a brand of cultural identity for the entire city.

Research results indicate that this campaign was part of a widespread trend, in Montreal and in the rest of the Canada – that of a corporate (hockey teams), popular (fans), and administrative (cities) desire to link city and hockey. A true fan "conquest" would be undertaken in the public space. To better understand the context of "The City Is Hockey" advertising campaign and the downtown roots of the Canadiens, this chapter addresses three main themes: the entry of hockey into the urban public space, or the "hockeyization" of Canadian cities; the desire to win the title of "hockeytown"; and the city's representation in the marketing of hockey in Montreal.[1]

We will examine the identity, socio-cultural, and above all urban quest that is part of the "hockeytown" system. This system is determined by four elements: hockeyization (the transfer of hockey into the urban space); "The City Is Hockey" (the Montreal advertising campaign); Hockeyville (a Canadian competition to decide which city in Canada has the biggest hockey fans); and hockeyitis (an insane passion for hockey). We will examine the links between the practice of hockey and the urban space, the exchanges between the practice of hockey and representations of the city, and, finally, the interrelations between hockey and representations of the city.

Between National Identity and Urban Identity

Hockey: The "Consolidator" of Canadian Identity

Beginning in the twentieth century, ice hockey spread throughout Canada and hockey became the national winter sport, an identity shared from sea to sea. The majority of Stanley Cups have been won by Canadian teams, and in spite of the internationalization of the NHL today, more than half the players in the league are from Canada. In a document on the future of NHL teams in Canada produced jointly by Industry Canada, the provinces, the municipalities, and the teams, the Public Policy Forum confirmed the impact and important role played by hockey in Canadian society (Public Policy Forum, 1999). It also talked about the historical and cultural impact of hockey: "Participants from all perspectives noted the prominent role that hockey – and professional hockey – has played in the history of Canada." For the participants in that forum, there was no question that hockey occupied a special place in Canadian life and in the mythology of its population, as the country's national winter sport. The same text mentions a statement from the NHL: "Canada is and always has been the heart of NHL hockey." The repeated victories of Team Canada in the Olympic Games, the World Championships, and the World Cup of Hockey since 2000, as well as the teams from Calgary, Edmonton, Ottawa, and Vancouver reaching the Stanley Cup playoffs in 2004, 2006, 2007, and 2011 respectively, have regenerated throughout Canada enthusiasm for hockey and pride in the national sport. Hockey is thus seen as at the heart of Canadian national identity.

According to a national survey conducted in March 1999 by Decima Research, 72 per cent of Canadians were of the opinion that hockey helped define them as Canadians. Similarly, in a national survey by *Maclean's* magazine asking them what were the things that brought them together, hockey came second, preceded only by the national health care system. What is more, the most important blog on hockey in the country has the evocative title Hockeynation, and the CBC has expressed the great importance of hockey in Canadian society by creating the Hockeyville competition. This competition, notable for the commitment and community spirit it generates, consists in choosing the strongest hockey community in the country. Communities throughout Canada compete with one another to show their passion for the game. In the first year of the competition, in 2006, 450 municipalities took part, proof positive of the interest in hockey outside the major urban centres and confirmation of the game's importance to Canadian society. Each year, the winning town receives $100,000 to renovate its sports facilities, as well as a chance to host an NHL pre-season game.[2] Roberval, Quebec, took advantage of its Hockeyville win in 2008 to refurbish its arena and create an Ice Village, which is now one of the main winter attractions in the town.

Hockey: An Urban Phenomenon

History tells us that hockey is primarily an urban phenomenon. In Montreal, the various arenas used by the professional teams, spread out across the city from east to west, show the hold that hockey has on the city. From the first skating rink built in 1862 and covered in 1875, south of St Catherine Street between Drummond and Stanley streets (the Victoria Skating Rink), to the Bell Centre located on Avenue des Canadiens-de-Montréal between de la Montagne and Stanley streets, location has always been a major factor in decisions to build an arena.[3]

The Montreal Amateur Athletic Association (MAAA), the National, the Montagnards, the Victorias, the Shamrocks, the Wanderers, the Maroons, and then the Canadiens were Montreal hockey teams, and their territory did not extend beyond the city limits. Until the beginning of the 1940s, hockey for Canadians remained essentially an urban phenomenon. As noted by François Black, "in that period, even though hockey was played even in the most remote corners of rural Quebec, the phenomenon of NHL professional hockey was mainly urban, if not to say metropolitan and more precisely Montreal" (1997, p. 57; translation). It was the gradual disappearance of those teams at the beginning of the twentieth century, especially of the Maroons in 1938, that made the Canadiens, now the only Montreal team, a provincial phenomenon: "once the team of the French Canadians, [it] would now be the team of all Montrealers, then the team of all of Quebec" (Black, 1997, p. 79; translation).

The "Hockeyization" of the City in Canada: the Rootedness of Hockey in the Urban Space

Previously confined to the arena, hockey and its rituals have gradually penetrated urban space through incentives put in place by various actors in the world of hockey. Cities in western Canada were the first to unofficially launch the hockeyization of the city. This phenomenon, which was only anecdotal a few years ago, has since become a tool for promotion and identification as well as a serious urban planning issue. There has been a sharing of appropriations: first hockey took support from the city, now the city takes support from hockey. Hockey has become a factor in urban identity. This phenomenon, beyond athletic and fan considerations, raises many questions for urban planning, related to these issues among others: noise management, urban security, access to public places, transportation, tourist infrastructure, and the building of facilities for public events. Let us look at how hockey has gradually invested the city.

Vancouver's "Towel Power"

In 1982, the Vancouver Canucks went on an improbable run to the Stanley Cup Finals. In the second game of the conference finals against the Chicago Blackhawks (29 April), head coach Roger Neilson grabbed a spare stick and hoisted it above his head with a towel hanging from it to protest the referee's calls (four straight penalties) against his team. Three players joined Neilson in his original way of saying "we surrender." This action and the booing from the crowd encouraged Vancouver entrepreneur Butts Giraud, owner of the Dog's Ear T-Shirt Boutique chain, to produce thousands of towels printed with the slogan, "Canucks Take No Survivors." During game three of the series, the first home game for the Canucks, 16,000 fans waved their white towels in the old Pacific Coliseum and launched the Towel Power phenomenon. "Towel Power" was raging so strongly that BC's Ministry of Tourism attempted to get in the *Guinness Book of World Records* by producing the world's longest towel, and had the entire BC Legislature sign it." Entrepreneur Giraud said it was "going to be bigger than the wave," and it created what is still today one of the most recognizable playoff traditions in sport – and, historically, a symbol of Canucks pride (http://canucks.nhl.com/club/news.htm?id=558295).

The Red Mile in Calgary: Hockey as Urban Promoter

It was in 1985 that hockey began to conquer urban space in the Canadian West, and all indications are that the process of hockeyization of the city is a growing phenomenon. During its series with the Winnipeg Jets, the Calgary Flames organization invited its fans to wear the red jersey of the team with its logo (the flaming C) to show their support. That was the beginning of the *C/Sea of Red*, today a major component of urban identity in Calgary. After Flames games, fans, who regularly numbered 100,000, would invade 11th Avenue SW, known then as "Electric Avenue." This phenomenon of the red tide was moved to 17th Avenue SW during the Stanley Cup playoffs in 2004. Now nicknamed the Red Mile by the mayor of the city (Eckler, 2004), the avenue is today inseparable from the image of hockey in Calgary and is a symbol of the city. The images of this hockeyized public space had been broadcast internationally on various media.

This appropriation of a public thoroughfare in the centre of the city had a significant impact on the renewal of Calgary's urban identity. The hockeyization of 17th Avenue was the beginning of a process of patrimonialization of that central artery, and the "Red Mile" since 2006 has been a registered trademark held by a private company. Like St. Lawrence Boulevard in Montreal, designated a national historic site by the Canadian government, 17th Avenue is now a known entity drawing its brand image mainly from the intangible. Today it has become a monument to Calgary's identity and a major tourist attraction. A website, www.theredmile.ca, site of the company Trilogy Promotion Inc., now http://theredmile.ca, promoted the avenue:

> You've heard about it on TV, you've read about it in the papers, and you've seen it on the Internet. NOW, come and visit it!
>
> With hundreds of local area merchants, our world famous Calgary hospitality, and a unique mix of historic and modern buildings, The Red Mile™ is a must-see shopping and tourism destination!

In its plans for the Red Mile, the promoter proposed the installation of webcams in order to broadcast live around the clock all the activity on 17th Avenue and make it a gathering place where hockey fans could encourage and celebrate their sports team. While hockeyization is a way to exploit the meaning given to that avenue, the promotion company also wants to benefit from it to attract the Other and the others, people who are not hockey enthusiasts: "For those who have visited the mile, you know that we aren't just about hockey; we are THE place to see and been seen."

During a survey titled "Imagine Calgary" on what makes Calgary a good place to live and what would make the city even more pleasant, the *Calgary Herald* wondered if the Red Mile had relevance in debates over urban design (Burgener, 2006). The answer was yes, especially when it came to public assemblies, citizenship, civility, celebrations, responsibility, spontaneity, and atmosphere.

The Calgary City Council met to develop a strategy aimed at striking a balance between liveability for residents, public safety, and the impact of bars near streets such as 17th Avenue and 1st Street SW (Derworiz, 2005). In 2005, councillor Madeleine King created the "17th Avenue Urban Design Strategy" by gathering together architects and landscapers. After public consultations, the development of the Red Mile as "a tree-lined boulevard with street cafes and low-rise buildings that combine condominiums and retail shops, bordering a series of urban parks" (Myers, 2006) was proposed.

During the celebrations of Alberta's centenary, the *Calgary Herald* presented a hundred of its historical front pages. The daily wrote that 2004 was the year Calgary became famous for its Red Mile (Marr and Spivak, 2005). The newspapers have widely promoted the term Red Mile since 2004, using it hundreds of times. In 2008, a huge sculpture of the Stanley Cup was erected downtown.

The Winnipeg White Out

Continuing the legacy of "Towel Power" and in reaction to the "*C of Red*," the Winnipeg Jets organization replied by creating the *Winnipeg White Out* and by asking the population to wear only white clothes during home games. The effect was gripping: "Winnipeg White-Out, literally a sea of 15,000 fans draped often in white sheets, white towels and white body paint, and always, in unrelenting pride. If nothing more, the franchise attracted hockey fans with co-ordination unmatched by any other NHL city" (Leipsic, 2004).

This gesture signified solidarity with the team. The fame of Winnipeg's white winters definitely played a role in the choice of colour. The tradition began in April 1985, far beyond the walls of the Winnipeg Arena: "The tradition evolved and fans were no longer simply wearing white at home games. When the team was on the road, fans gathered at various establishments, all wearing white ... It had struck a chord with the city and camaraderie amongst all fans and the team had been built" (Maniago, 2007).

During the playoffs, the centre of Winnipeg became the vessel of that white crowd, which gathered at the corner of Portage Avenue and Main Street. The tradition ended when the team moved to Phoenix.[4] Then, during the Stanley Cup final in 2004, Tampa Bay created a pale copy of the *Winnipeg White Out*, which lasted only a single season (Taylor, 2004). Finally, in 2008, the Pittsburgh Penguins, who played in the Mellon Arena, commonly nicknamed "the Igloo" because of its shape and colour, gave new life to the Winnipeg tradition on 25 April 2008, during a game against the New York Rangers.[5] The tradition is now well established during playoffs in Pittsburgh. These are three examples of ephemeral events that gave life to urban space without affecting the form or designation. They represent the early stages of hockeyization.

Edmonton Blue Mile: From Virtual Space to Public Space

The Edmonton Oilers, in their bid for the Stanley Cup in 2006, launched a movement similar to the ones in Calgary and Winnipeg by promoting the wearing of blue jerseys during home games. The Edmonton media nicknamed Whyte Avenue the "Blue Mile" to reflect the fans' appropriation of an artery symbolically linked to the Oilers: "Thousands of fans marched up and down the so-called 'Blue Mile'"; "Whyte Avenue is to become Edmonton's Blue Mile version of Calgary's Red Mile." (Canadian Press, 2006; Macafee, Canadian Press, 2006). This avenue quickly became a favourite gathering place in the city. The creation of the Bluemile.ca website enhanced the development of this identity through the dissemination of images of activities along Whyte Avenue. More than a place to celebrate hockey, the Blue Mile is now a place for festivities: very particular rituals are staged in this public space in the heart of Edmonton.[6] The media campaign and the Web contributed to this appropriation of Whyte Avenue.

The Sens Mile in Ottawa: The Domino Effect and the Magic of Facebook

Hockey also conquered the street in the national capital when the Ottawa Senators made the Stanley Cup finals in 2007. Decrying the lack of public enthusiasm for his city's team, Shane Currey, a nineteen-year-old Ottawan, posted a call on Facebook to take to the streets. One fan said: "Calgary did it in the streets. Edmonton did it in the streets. We want the nation to know we support our team" (Desaulniers, 2007). The resulting Facebook group, "I Am an Ottawa Senators Fan," with more than 15,000 members, was an unparalleled launch pad for the creation of a "Sens Mile." It was inaugurated virtually on 15 May 2007 to gather Ottawans on Elgin Street at the corner of McLaren. On 16 May, the Facebook page received coverage in the Ottawa and Montreal dailies, and the process of hockeyization had begun (Brodie, 2007; *Ottawa Sun*, 2007). Two days later, the project won the support of the city's mayor. The *Ottawa Citizen* reported that the mayor, Larry O'Brien, might give his approval to designate as "Sens Mile" a section of Elgin Street if the team reached the Stanley Cup finals (Desaulniers, 2007). The first major appropriation of the street took place on 19 May, when Ottawa eliminated Buffalo: "Sens Mile – an Elgin Street fan zone similar to Calgary's Red Mile and Edmonton's Whyte Avenue – was baptized yesterday" (Deachman, 2007). On 28 May, the first day of the Stanley Cup final, the city was busy putting up new signs with the name Sens Mile on Elgin Street. In the space of a week, the Sens Mile was born and strongly established in the city and in the collective consciousness (Sadava, 2007).

Montreal and the Blue–White–Red Wave

A new ritual was born in 2008 in Montreal: the display of the Habs pennant on vehicles. Already well established in Toronto, this custom spread like wildfire during the playoffs: 5,000 miniature flags were sold every day for a total of nearly 200,000. The entire metropolitan region was decorated with the mobile symbol. In Montreal, hockeyization was not concentrated in one place; it spread throughout the downtown. Along Crescent, de la Montagne, Drummond, and St Catherine streets, the blue–white–red was displayed in the windows of clothes boutiques, on the terraces of restaurants, on the doors and facades of buildings, on lampposts, and even on fire halls. A Tricolore wave was unfurled over downtown Montreal on game days and spilled onto La Gauchetière Street (now Avenue des Canadiens-de-Montréal), St Catherine Street, and René-Lévesque Boulevard after a victory.

In Victoria Square, Guillaume Pharand and Jean-Luc Lavallée, two fans with sewing skills, stitched together an enormous Canadiens jersey and dressed the sculpture by the artist Ju Ming in it. That statue, *Taichi Single Whip*, became during the playoffs a symbol of hockey.

This Tricolore wave was repeated with as much fervour during the 2010 playoffs. The elimination of the Washington Capitals and the Pittsburgh Penguins in two seven-game series generated monster rallies in downtown Montreal. On game days, the Montreal police closed Avenue-des-Canadiens-de-Montréal and St Catherine Street to car traffic.

Hockeytown: Defending the Title of Hockey Capital

The question of what really is a "hockeytown" has been debated for years without any consensus being achieved. Journalist Terry Frei attempted in 2006 to define the term (2006). For him, it is mainly about people's enthusiasm for the game, evidenced by their deep knowledge of it and by the presence of many skating rinks where they actually play it.[7] In real hockeytowns, the population gets excited about the sport – something measured by team loyalty and by attendance at games. Hockey has to be at the centre of the city's concerns, and when the team makes the playoffs, the streets have to be transformed (hockey-ized) with team colours to make way for a succession of citizen rituals known collectively as "playoff fever."

We suggest adding another three attributes. The city's team must have a long history of winning; enthusiasm for hockey should not be ephemeral but rather perennial; and a street or square must be designated to accommodate the various public demonstrations associated with hockey.

Hockeytown, New York: Buffalo

Montreal has attempted to affirm itself as *the* hockeytown in order to compete with cities (like Edmonton and Calgary) that have appropriated that label for themselves or that aspire to do so. Minnesota, home of the Minnesota Wild (based in St Paul), has proclaimed itself the "State of Hockey," a tradition going back to the North Stars and the Minnesota State team of the 1970s. In 2007, the *New York Times* reported that Buffalo had proposed calling itself "another hockeytown"; according to that same report, *ESPN Magazine* had called the Buffalo Sabres "the ultimate sports franchise, ahead of even the Red Wings – standard-bearers for hockey success in the United States" (Higgins, 2007).

The *Buffalo News* confirmed the spread of a "playoff fever" and did not hesitate to call Buffalo a "real hockeytown" (Herrmann, 2007). But hockey's grip on Buffalo cannot be compared with that on cities in western Canada. Buffalo's "Parties in the Plaza" on HSBC Plaza – gatherings of fans watching games together wearing yellow and blue – more closely resemble the pre-game "tailgate parties" that take place in the parking lots of NFL stadiums. For the 2014–15 playoffs, the New York Rangers adopted the moniker "Rangerstown Hockey House." A Web platform has been created for fans to show their appreciation for the team; in addition, a physical meeting place allows fans to gather near Madison Square Garden at Herald Square, where large letters that spell out RANGERSTOWN have been installed. This contributes to inscribing hockey on the city and consecrating New York as a hockey town.

Hockeytown, Michigan: Detroit

Currently, only one city in North America is "officially" a hockeytown: Detroit. The Red Wings are the best American team of all time, having won the Stanley Cup eleven times. In 1996, Detroit registered the trademark "Hockeytown" for the Joe Louis Arena and the franchise. This designation was strengthened by the arrival of strong players (the "Russian Five") who revitalized the club in the early 1990s. The city has thus been recognized as "*the* hockeytown."

But however important Detroit is as an ambassador city for hockey in the United States, that designation will surprise some. Its more popular nickname, Motor City, is well earned, but its claim to be *the* hockeytown have been questioned by both players and the media. Over the past few years, hundreds of playoff tickets have gone unsold in the city.[8] Red Fischer, a journalist at the Montreal *Gazette*, wrote: "We're not talking New Jersey here, where empty seats have become a rule, rather than an exception. We're talking about Hockeytown, U.S.A. The Detroit Red Wings, for heaven's sake!" (Fischer, 2007a). The newspaper headlines were explicit: "Cup Generates Very Little Buzz" (Fischer, 2007b); "Bye, Bye Hockeytown?" (Sharp, 2006). As Larry Wigge (2002) pointed out in the *Sporting News*, "Where is Hockeytown? Detroit isn't the only city that makes a strong claim to being the center of the ice universe – NHL" (2002).

Hockey today is a brand name that brings fame. Cities and hockey fans try to set themselves apart; to mark their identity, they develop rituals and designations their city recognizes.

Hockeytown, Quebec: Montreal

In March 1996, the McCord Museum opened the exhibition *Montreal, That's Hockey*, which told the 120-year history of that winter sport. In a poll conducted by the TSN network to identify *the* Canadian hockeytown, Montreal came out ahead. In another survey, this one of NHL players for *Sports Illustrated*, Montrealers were declared, with a comfortable lead, "the best fans in the NHL." The same poll confirmed Canadian fans' enthusiasm for their teams, especially in the West: five of the six first places were occupied by Canadian teams.

For former Canadiens player Guy Lafleur, "Montreal is one of the most remarkable hockeytowns in the world. Perhaps the most exceptional, in fact. The fans encourage their team like nowhere else and they help to boost the reputation of the city throughout North America" (Lafleur, 2008; translation). Montreal is thus the city that corresponds best to a "hockeytown." It is in Montreal that this sport was invented in the second half of the nineteenth century and where "the first real hockey game was played on 3 March 1875 at the Victoria Skating Rink" (Black, 1997, p. 19; translation). Ron MacLean, former host of *Hockey Night in Canada* on the CBC, refers to Montreal as "the cradle of organized sport." It is in Montreal, at the Windsor Hotel, that the NHL was founded, on 26 November 1917. The Canadiens have won the most championships and Stanley Cups (twenty-four). It is "the greatest team in the history of hockey" (Black, 1997, p. 19; translation), based in "the hockey capital of the world"; it is the "greatest dynasty" in the sport (Fischler and Richard, 1971, p. 3; translation). Montreal has the largest arena in the NHL. Since 8 January 2004, all home games have been sold out (more than three hundred). The recent and projected successes of the team recall its glorious past and allow Montreal, the Mecca of professional hockey (Bourque, 1996, p. 7), to take full ownership of the brand "hockeytown." The death of Le Gros Bill, Jean Béliveau, has left an empty seat, which will remain so for the rest of the 2014–15 season. A light beam from the ceiling lights his seat, which is covered with his number 4 jersey, a powerful symbol of his presence.

Hockey needs a street or a place to "show" itself, an urban space that can be hockeyized. In Montreal, St Catherine Street has always been the main artery for spontaneous demonstrations. When they moved from the Forum to their new arena, the Canadiens created a new semi-public place, Windsor Court, to accommodate thousands of fans, with a structure that can serve as a giant screen for broadcasting games. But it is Avenue des Canadiens-de-Montréal, a narrow street with little traffic, that serves as the plaza for the Bell Centre. It is where fans gather after wins by the Habs before heading to St Catherine Street. Columnist Bertrand Raymond of the *Journal de Montréal* suggested its name be changed to "Place Maurice-Richard" (Raymond, 2006); three years later, however, during the city's centennial celebrations, it was renamed Avenue des Canadiens-de-Montréal.

Centennial Plaza

On 4 December 2008, the ninety-ninth anniversary of the founding of the Canadiens, a new semi-public square adjoining the Bell Centre was opened, Centennial Plaza. The site had been an asphalt lot with a passageway leading to the train station and the Bell Centre side entrance. Commemorating one hundred years of Canadiens history, it includes four monuments to former players (Howie Morenz, Maurice Richard, Jean Béliveau, and Guy Lafleur), fifteen plaques commemorating the players whose jerseys had been retired, one hundred sidewalk plaques recalling the greatest moments in the club's history, and a monument honouring the 761 players who had played for the Habs. Erected at the centre of Centennial Plaza, this monument recalls not only the names of the players but also the names of the coaches and general managers throughout the history of the team as well as the recipients of individual trophies awarded by the NHL. This historical list is completed by the annual records of the Canadiens for each of their first hundred seasons (1909–2009).

The Canadiens' marketing department meant this site to honour the legends and to serve a gathering place and assembly point for fans:

> It was to mark with great pomp the 100 years of the Montreal Canadiens and to leave behind a unique sports heritage for all the fans of the team that Centennial Plaza was created, a veritable open-air museum where the history of the Tricolore is forever inscribed in stone ... The primary goal was to give a wonderful gift, an historical legacy, to the fans while continuing the beautification of the Bell Centre and its surroundings. (Daigneault, 2008, p. 8; translation)

Centennial Plaza is an educational and interactive space. Twenty thousand personalized bricks cover the square. With the campaign "Immortalize your place in the history of the Canadians with Centennial Plaza," the club encouraged fans to buy a brick and write on it a brief message. The terms and conditions for the purchase of a brick recall that this square belongs to and is managed by the Canadiens hockey club. Some excerpts:

> In order to preserve the integrity of Centennial Plaza, all messages [written on a brick] must be linked to the history of the Montreal Canadiens.
>
> The bricks placed in Centennial Plaza are the property of the Canadiens hockey club, Inc. Buyers have no property rights to the bricks placed in Centennial Plaza.
>
> The location of Centennial Plaza is subject to change. It is understood that the Canadiens Hockey Club Inc. does not guarantee the preservation of Centennial Plaza beyond 1 June 2018.
>
> The exact location, design, appearance, construction, installation, maintenance and repair of the bricks will be at the sole discretion of the Canadiens Hockey Club Inc.

At any hour of the day, people, many wearing Canadiens jerseys, would stop in front of the monuments or the bricks to be photographed or to observe, read, or contemplate a piece of the history of the Canadiens. Before the plaza was created, this square had been the site of pre-game activities, the Fan Jam. Until the 2011–12 season, thousands of fans displaying the Tricolore would gather before games, especially during the playoffs, in an atmosphere that was, to say the least, highly charged.

On 16 July 2012, the Canadiens management announced with its partners[9] that a forty-eight-floor condo would be constructed on the site of Centennial Plaza. With the building of the "Tour des Canadiens," the highest residential tower in the city, the square will have vanished less than four years after it was opened.

The square, which had been funded largely by fans, was dismantled, and all the statues, plaques, monuments, and bricks were placed in temporary storage for "as long as it takes to design a new square" (Radio-Canada, 2012; translation). According to Geoff Molson, owner of the Canadiens, "the concept of the Centennial Plaza [would] be maintained as well as the name" and the administration would work on "finding them a nice location" (Rioux, 2012; translation). Here is an excerpt from the message sent to the people who had bought centennial bricks on the very day the "Tour des Canadiens" was opened:

> La Tour des Canadiens will be erected on Centennial Plaza, the space where thousands of bricks purchased by fans such as yourself ahead of the club's 100th anniversary are currently on display. We wanted to reach out

to each and every one of you because we can appreciate the importance of the gesture you made when you ordered your brick several years ago; you not only paid homage to the ties and passion you and/or your loved ones have for the Canadiens, but you helped directly fund the very construction of Centennial Plaza itself.

Please rest assured that until your brick can be reintegrated into the environment surrounding the new residential complex, it will be carefully removed from Centennial Plaza and stored along with all others at a secure facility. We will ensure that your brick remains preserved in its current state without incident throughout any phase of construction that would otherwise risk damaging what we are sure is an important symbol of your attachment to the Canadiens.

As an organization, it is of critical importance for us to ensure all of Centennial Plaza's components – your bricks, the statues honoring our legends, and the surrounding elements – all remain in pristine condition throughout the construction period and are reintegrated in a seamless, appropriate manner within the new space. The project's developers are equally committed in that regard as it is clear these elements are what will help make La Tour des Canadiens and the Bell Centre one of downtown Montreal's premiere destinations.

We will keep you abreast of developments in the coming months. Know that your contribution will always be an important part of Montreal Canadiens history.[10]

In spite of these reassuring comments, there was uncertainty about the location, the form, and the timing of new Centennial Plaza. The bricks and the commemorative space would not be accessible to the public before 2015, the planned date for the completion of the building. In addition, with the construction of the Deloitte Tower (26 storeys) on a portion of Windsor Court, and of L'Avenue (50 storeys) in front of the Bell Centre, the options for re-establishing Centennial Plaza were narrowing. The prestige of the Canadiens and their marketing strategy had shifted to the sale of luxury condos; the monetary and emotional investment of the fans in Centennial Plaza had been pushed to the background.

A decision was finally taken in 2013. "Slated to open in 2016 alongside the new Tour Deloitte office tower, the next iteration of Centennial Plaza will be found on the eastern part of the Bell Centre – outdoors and adjacent to Windsor Court and the Montreal Canadiens Hall of Fame" (http://canadiens.nhl.com/club/news.htm?id=672512

#&navid=MTL-search). "In recent months there had been much discussion as to how the Plaza would be re-incorporated into the Bell Centre environs with the multitude of construction projects in the immediate vicinity, yet Canadiens owner Geoff Molson laid to rest all speculation in unveiling the striking vision for what is effectively considered the team's 'outdoor museum'" (http://canadiens.nhl.com/club/news.htm?id=672512#&navid=MTL-search).

The new space will include all the former elements of the Centennial Plaza and "promises to be a popular oasis at the heart of the downtown core" even if no or very few amenities such as trees, benches, water features, and so on are planned. The plaza will remain a place of representation rather than a facility for improving the lives of downtown Montrealers.

Avenue des Canadiens-de-Montréal

As part of the centenary celebrations, the Canadiens and the City of Montreal jointly decided, with the approval of the Commission de toponymie du Québec (Toponymy Commission of Quebec) (CTQ), to rename the stretch of La Gauchetière Street between Peel and de la Montagne streets. This part of the street runs alongside the Bell Centre and faces Centennial Plaza (Clément, 2008; Mathieu, 2009). Avenue des Canadiens-de-Montréal, unveiled on 9 October 2009 and made official by the CTQ on 15 April 2010, is a new toponymic designation evoking the social heritage of the team.[11]

Avenue des Canadiens-de-Montréal is the first public roadway in Quebec to carry the name of a sports team. However, across Quebec, many streets, parks, and lakes are named in honour of former Canadiens players (Champagne, 2010). This is especially visible in Vaudreuil-Dorion, where all the streets in one part of the town have names connected to the team (Toe-Blake, Léo-Gravel, Aurèle-Joliat, Elmer-Lach, Édouard-Lalonde, Howie-Morenz, Jacques-Plante, Claude-Provost, Maurice-Richard and Frank-Selke streets).[12]

An avenue is usually a wide street lined with trees, often leading to a prestigious place or building. In Montreal, Morgan, Bernard, and De Lorimier avenues are in keeping with this definition. In the case at hand, the famous narrow stretch of street has none of the characteristics of an avenue, except for being lined with important buildings. The built environment of the Avenue des Canadiens-de-Montréal includes the Bell Centre, home of the Canadiens since 1996; 1250 René-Lévesque

(IBM-Marathon), the second-highest skyscraper in Montreal and recipient of the Orange Prize by Save Montreal; and St George Anglican Church and Windsor Station, both of which are National Historic Monuments.

Avenue des Canadiens-de-Montréal, which pays homage to the team that has won the most Stanley Cups, intersects Stanley Street, a coincidence that heightens the new name's symbolism. So despite the disappearance of the Centennial Plaza, this part of the city is still clearly identified with the Tricolore.

Hockey and City: The Association of Downtown Montreal with the Canadiens

The representation of the city in the marketing of hockey in Montreal began tentatively at the end of the 1980s with *Les Canadiens*, the official magazine of the Montreal hockey club. Many players were photographed in front of emblematic urban buildings and landscapes.[13] During the 1993 playoffs, *La Presse* hired caricaturist André Pijet to represent the Canadiens' quest for the Stanley Cup. Starting with the first series between the Canadiens and the Nordiques, Pijet evoked the architectural symbols in the Montreal–Quebec City duel. For example, the Olympic Stadium fighting the Château Frontenac, with the two buildings wearing the jerseys of their respective teams. In the series against the New York Islanders, landmark buildings in Manhattan took on the Canadiens players. For Pijet, clearly, hockey was more than a sport; it was an expression of urban societies vying with one another.

During television broadcasts of hockey games, it is customary, whatever the network, to show images of the downtown skyline of the city where the match is being played. Recent airings of Canadiens games on the RDS sports network have offered a visual montage in which the puck flies through the downtown core, weaving through skyscrapers to finally enter through the roof of 1000 de La Gauchetière and bounce off the ice in the Bell Centre. These various manifestations are related to symbolic images; the downtown, through its skyscrapers, appears as a distinctive urban brand connected to hockey. The current presentation projects giant Habs players (former and current) across and in front of the city's most prominent buildings (Maurice Richard and Notre-Dame Basilica, Guy Lafleur and the Olympic Stadium, Jean Béliveau and the Jacques-Cartier Bridge, Patrick Roy and the Champlain Bridge, Larry Robinson and the CIBC Tower, Andrei Markov and 1250

René-Lévesque, Brian Gionta and Place Ville Marie). To this is added a view of the intersection of Peel Street and De Maisonneuve Boulevard with, in the foreground, a poster column displaying Ken Dryden, among others.

The process of associating the city with hockey entered a decisive phase in 1993, when construction of the new arena began. The ground for it was broken in June 1993; the Molson Centre opened in March 1996. This was a major urban revitalization project in the heart of the downtown. It was important from the start to "integrate this recreational structure into the urban fabric" (*Le magazine Centre Molson*, p. 45):

> To the initial challenge was added that of integrating the new temple of the Glorieux into downtown. It is a hub around which all kinds of activities would gravitate, and other elements that would be attached to it. (*Le magazine Centre Molson*, p. 27)
>
> The plan to upgrade one of the most prestigious blocks in downtown Montreal includes a rail station of heritage interest. In addition to the construction of a new 21,500-seat arena and renovations to the historic station, the project includes connecting two subway stations, the creation of a public square, "the Windsor Court," a suburban train terminal and a sophisticated communications system. (*Le magazine Centre Molson*, p. 37; translation)

The site's location in the "middle of downtown" (*Le magazine Centre Molson*, p. 45), the ease of access, and the creation of a hub for the city that would play a role in urban development besides meeting the needs of the hockey club, all had an impact on the project and associated the city more than ever with hockey. "Located in the heart of the city, west of the block bounded by the streets La Gauchetière, Saint-Antoine, Peel and the mountain, the new forum will be quickly accessible by the Ville-Marie expressway or by major city streets" (Canadiens Hockey Club, 1996, p. 2; translation). In short, "all roads lead to the Molson Centre" (*Le magazine Centre Molson*, p. 45; translation).

For the chairman of Molson, this project was "the cornerstone of the revitalization of downtown Montreal, beside recently completed buildings and office towers that will rise up when the complex is completed" (Molson, 1996, p. 210; translation). In their publicity documents, the Canadiens blended tradition and modernity by speaking of a new temple of hockey. "Rising among the modern towers of the downtown and the historic Windsor Station, the new Forum will quickly impose itself as the focal point of Montreal, as the reflection of our sense of pride. This masterpiece of urban architecture ... with its dynamic, contemporary design ... harmonizes with the environment and the urban setting" (Canadiens Hockey Club, 1996, p. 1; translation).

Architectural Representations of Montreal in the Marketing of Hockey

To reconnect with fans after the lockout in the 2004–5 season, the Canadiens tried to develop a more direct relationship with them while broadening its target audience.[14] Hockey was going to go beyond its solely athletic image; it would be represented as Montreal's identity. The city and the urban landscape would become instruments of promotion, points of reference taking part in the revitalization of hockey. After the "partisan heureux" ("happy fan") advertising campaign in 2003–4 and the "Tricolore jusqu'au bout" ("Tricolore to the end") campaign in 2005–6, the club's marketing department was looking for a strong and simple slogan that would combine two facets of Montreal: its urban environment, and hockey. It was certain that the two went hand in hand. Restoring a winning, vital image to the Canadiens would have direct repercussions for the city. Given that Montreal is the only francophone market in the NHL and that hockey is the number one entertainment value in Montreal and in Quebec, it was important for the marketing team "to put forward our culture, our heritage." The objectives were to show that hockey was again being played in the city, to generate passion for hockey and for the players, and to "convert" young people into fans of the Tricolore. The text of the television advertising was as follows: "Like a shock wave that connects the whole city. Everything is now being prepared to be experienced at the same pace. The team is prime for action. The 7th player is everywhere. The city is hockey" (translation). This message evoked a surge of hockey fever, spreading from a precise point, the Bell Centre, and generating a city-wide vibration. Hockey was presented as a unifying factor for the city and its people, one that enlarged the urban boundaries. This advertising, widely broadcast and extended during the 2007–8 and 2008–9 seasons, strongly merged city and hockey. The campaign was shown before every game on the electronic scoreboard and even projected on the ice surface, besides being broadcast at the beginning of the season on the RDS and TVA television networks, on Astral billboards along streets and highways, on Morris columns downtown, in *Le Journal de Montréal*, the *Gazette*, and *Métro*, and in La Cage aux Sports restaurants.

The campaign's orientation was clear, whatever the context: hockey fever was going to conquer the whole city. City and hockey would join together in promoting the metropolis. Highly expressive ads placed images of players against the background of the city. The players in red jerseys brought movement and dynamism; the pale buildings stood out against a blue sky. This campaign aimed to restore lustre to the Canadiens using powerful symbols as well as carefully selected landmark buildings. The ultimate objective, according to the sponsors, was to declare: "Le hockey, c'est nous, Montréal, c'est nous, le Québec" ("Hockey is us, Montreal is us, Quebec") (Prunier, 2007). The campaign succeeded: "The city is hockey" became a widespread expression in everyday language,[15] and the Canadiens logo could be seen everywhere in the city and beyond, on jerseys, posters, flags, and merchandise. Even the city buses displayed "Go Habs Go" above their windshields. Many restaurants, shops, and buildings – even fire halls – flew the Tricolore. Like "Hockeytown," "Red Mile," "Blue Mile" and "Sens Mile," "The City Is Hockey" has become part of the quest for a designation specific to Montreal, and as such, it has participated clearly in the phenomenon of hockeyization in Montreal.

The architectural representations of the city chosen for the ad campaign can be divided into three categories: the emblems of the metropolis, the eight downtown skyscrapers, and the temple of hockey.

The emblems of the metropolis include the Bonsecours Market (1847), the Roddick Gate of McGill University (1925), the Jacques-Cartier Bridge (1930), the central building of the Université de Montréal (1943), and the Biosphere, the former American pavilion at Expo 67. These are symbols of Montreal society. They evoke the geographic and territorial location of Montreal, since they stand respectively in Old Montreal, in the downtown, on the St. Lawrence River, on Mount Royal, and on St. Helen's Island. They are located at the centre of the island of Montreal, and their silhouettes stand out because of their elevation or their isolation. The buildings chosen express the city's architectural diversity, which includes neoclassical, Art Deco, and modern styles. The Bonsecours Market with its dome, which represents the old character of the metropolis, remains the "ancestor of the major multifunctional buildings in Montreal" (Gauthier and Bisson, 1990, p. 149; translation). The former American pavilion asserts the technological progress and innovation characterized by the 1967 World's Fair. Like Expo 67, the emblems of Montreal embody openness to the world, the export of models, Quebec know-how, dialogue between francophones and anglophones, and even links with the suburbs.

The eight downtown skyscrapers, grouped in a very limited area, seem to be the city's main identifying element. The buildings represented are Place Ville Marie (1962), the BNP-Paribas Tower (1981), the Laurentienne Bank Tower (1984), the KPMG Tower (1988), 1501 McGill College (1992), the 1000 De La Gauchetière (1992), 1250 René-Lévesque (1993), and E-Commerce Place (2003). Height is a major component in the choice of the buildings: four of the highest skyscrapers in the metropolis are included. Place Ville Marie is included as the highest point in the city (because of the rising topography of downtown, from the river to the mountain), beside two taller buildings, 1000 De La Gauchetière (205 metres) and 1250 René-Lévesque (199 metres).

The locations of the skyscrapers selected for advertisement follow two main axes that evoke the layout of the city. The east–west René Lévesque–La Gauchetière axis and the north–south McGill College–University axis share the architectural objects, each with four buildings. The east–west axis expresses the immediate context of the Bell Centre, the heart of hockey in Montreal. As for 1000 De La Gauchetière, its position on the same street as the Bell Centre, its indoor skating rink, and its altitude make it a flagship building associated with the temple of hockey, along with 1250 René-Lévesque, which, besides recalling the Chrysler Building with its romantic elegance, opens its urban square on Windsor Court. The glass walls of the skyscrapers frame the Bell Centre and make it stand out, creating a sense of strength and power. The north–south axis represents the symbolic heart of downtown Montreal. Place Ville Marie is the "symbol of the modern city [and] its shopping mall ... was the starting point for Montreal's underground pedestrian network" (Gauthier and Bisson, 1990, p. 144; translation). The KPMG Tower and 1501 McGill College are landmark buildings in the downtown thanks to their unusual shapes (pyramid-shaped upper floors and "cat ears"), their colouring, their use of light, and their key locations. The skyscrapers thus evoke the dominant axes of the street grid, the entrance into modernity of the city, institutional power, and the quest for summits. Even more significantly, the buildings' locations create two major poles downtown: the central pole of the city, around Place Ville Marie, and the central pole of hockey, around the Bell Centre.

The temple of hockey, our third category, has only one building – the "new Forum," the Bell Centre (1996). Such an advertising presence is obviously aimed at establishing the building's renown a decade after the team moved into that structure. The "ghosts" of the Forum are slowly finding their niches in the Bell Centre, and the population is beginning to give the building symbolic value. Publicizing the Bell's Centre's image as the new Mecca of hockey, as embodying that sport and its greatest team, helps stimulate the public's imagination. Hockey permeates the city, but it is played at the Bell Centre. Along with the Jacques Cartier Bridge, the biosphere, and Place Ville Marie, the Bell Centre is the building most often represented in Canadiens advertising. While promoting hockey, the bridge, the geodesic dome, and the cruciform tower – three of the most powerful symbols of the Montreal urban identity – affirm, along with other elements chosen for the campaign, the city's pride, dynamism, and cultural richness.

Montreal lives to the rhythm of hockey, and the sport's image is now inseparable from the city's. The "City Is Hockey" campaign, which is based on the downtown's architectural framework, continues a profound quest, for prestige, success, and performance.

From Calgary to Montreal, hockey has penetrated urban space and urban planning. Whether through informal appropriation or specific designation, hockeyization transforms cities and associates hockey with defined spaces. In Montreal, this phenomenon has consecrated the link between the metropolis and hockey and expressed a quest to develop a unique urban identity. In 2014–15, the Canadiens launched the "Club 1909" fan program, an initiative aimed at uniting fans of the team around the world ("Unite the Faithful") in order to promote the team globally. Meanwhile an advertising campaign continues to forge the Montreal's identity as hockeytown with the slogan: "Le club du hockey," a variation of "The City is Hockey."

NOTES

1 The research leading to the association of hockey and city was carried out from 2004 to 2008. Canadian and American newspapers from some fifteen cities and advertising documents from the marketing department of the Canadiens hockey club were the main sources. To these were added analyses from a few Web sources, in particular Wiki articles, blogs and especially content-sharing platforms such as Facebook, which are major public forums for hockey fans in North America.

2 The winning municipalities were Salmon Shores, Nova Scotia (2006), North Bay, Ontario (2007), Roberval, Quebec (2008), Terrace, British Columbia (2009), Dundas, Ontario (2010), Conception Bay South, Newfoundland and Labrador (2011), Stirling-Rawdon, Ontario (2012), and Sylvan Lake, Alberta (2014).

3 The arenas used by the Canadiens are as follows: 1909–1910 and 1918–1919: Jubilee Arena (Sainte-Catherine/Moreau Station); 1910–1918: Westmount Arena (Sainte-Catherine/Wood); 1919–1926: Mount Royal Arena (Mount Royal/St. Urbain); 1926–1996: Forum (Sainte-Catherine/Atwater); since 1996: Bell Centre (La Gauchetière/de la Montagne).

4 The return of the Jets to Winnipeg for the 2011–12 season would contribute to a strong comeback of the *White Out*.

5 This initiative by the organization, which took up the term "*White Out*," was launched by a video clip on Facebook and on the website of the team on 24 April 2008. The organization provided all viewers with a T-shirt and a towel.

6 A Calgary journalist called into question the authenticity of the Edmonton Blue Mile in relations to the Red Mile in Calgary (Fortney, 2006).

7 The fans must have knowledge of the history of the players on the team and the ambitions of the organization, follow the activities of all the NHL teams, know the nationalities of players, and have a detailed understanding of the rules.

8 In spite of Stanley Cup wins in 1997, 1998, 2002 and 2008.

9 Cadillac Fairview, Canderel and the Fond Immobilier de Solidarité FTQ (real estate investment fund of the FTQ union federation).

10 Message from the Canadiens hockey club sent to centennial brick holders, 16 July 2012 (http://canadiens.nhl.com/club/news.htm?id=637994).

11 The origin and meaning of the designation, according to the CTQ, is as follows: "On 4 December 2009, the Montreal Canadiens team became the first team in the National Hockey League to celebrate 100 years of existence. In the context of the celebrations around this event, the City of Montreal approved a part of the street called La Gauchetière West be identified by the name Avenue des Canadiens-de-Montreal. The Bell Centre, where the club's matches have been played since 1996, is located there." Source: http://toponymie.gouv.qc.ca/ct/accueil.aspx

12 These names related to the Canadiens hockey club were made official by the CTQ in 2005.

13 With five to seven issues published each year since the 1985–1986 season, the magazine now has the name *Canadiens*. In 1988, Stéphane Richer was photographed downtown in front of the sculpture *The Illuminated Crowd*

on McGill College Avenue. The next year, Russian Courtnall was photographed in various places in Old Montreal, in particular in front of the clock tower. In 1991, Mathieu Schneider was shown at a "arrêt/stop" sign, a very Montreal feature, as well as in front of a skyscraper. Then in 1992, it was the turn of Vincent Damphousse to be photographed with the signs for Atwater Avenue and Sainte-Catherine Street, as well as on the lookout on Mount Royal with its view of the downtown skyscrapers.

14 The research that has made it possible for me to write this section was done in collaboration with the marketing department of the Canadiens hockey club. We would like to especially thank Jonathan Prunier and Mathieu Lapointe.

15 The expression is now well established in the Montreal identity. The phrase is constantly repeated in the sports and general media. A special program aired in April 2008 on the specialty channel RIS was entitled "the city is hockey."

7 "Bread and Circuses": Reading Juvenal in Montreal

ALAIN DENEAULT

It is as if the billboards in the city read: "Hockey is the opium of the people!" As if the crowd itself were chanting: "Bread! Circuses! Bread! Circuses! ..." This is "The City Is Hockey." This is what Montreal calls itself, and Quebec City, its rival, can only reply with a "blue march" policy, which calls for the creation of an unlikely sports venue, the new Colisée, which is now, in 2015, near completion. We even have a theologian who devotes his pious meditations to the circus (Bauer, 2011). What reflections does this stimulate? Do we truly need to consider the political meaning of childish rallying cries?

"The City Is Hockey" ... This sports marketing slogan has been drummed into us since 2006. It still gets close to 50,000 hits (many recent) when you word-search "Montreal" on the Internet, and it reflects a social phenomenon throughout the continent – many urban centres hope to enhance their self-image by "hockeyizing the city."[1] Long before self-satisfied slogans like this one came into vogue, there were some critics of the practice. Juvenal today would have declared it "difficult to not write satires." In the decadent period when *Rome was circus*, that polemicist had depicted his city in terms of sports and easy money. His *Satires* from the second century AD – to which we owe the proverbial expression "bread and circuses" – reveal striking similarities with to our era. They remind us that sports, as a spectacle occupying the heart of the city, are aimed more at cutting us off from urban life than at connecting us to it. They entail shifting the social dynamics to an artificial register that is capable of neutralizing them. The city can then see itself "as hockey" as much as it wants; though so long as it carries out the ontological production of the cliché "Bread! Circuses!," it will not make itself *more* of a city.

It would be mistake to reduce Juvenal's *Satires* to misogynous, xenophobic caricatures or to ill-tempered denunciations of a world abandoning its morals. Or to read them simply as diatribes against an order in which money dominates social relationships and corrupts minds; in which society's rules have been turned upside down; in which the masters, obsessed with ostentatious spending, leave their slaves to suffer in the cold; in which life on credit is based precariously on a meagre and endlessly mortgaged heritage; in which hooligans are honoured; in which the men dress as women and women talk like men; in which pretentiousness confidently reigns; and in which all social codes are disrupted ... Indeed, in which a *carnivalization* of the world takes the place of collective relationships:

> Why tell how my heart burns dry with rage when I see the people hustled by a mob of retainers attending on one who has defrauded and debauched his ward, or on another who has been condemned by a futile verdict – for what matters infamy if the cash be kept? (Satire 1, pp. 45–48; all quotations of Juvenal are from. G.G. Ramsay's translation)

Moreover, with regard to the central position of the circus in the city, Juvenal describes a moment of collective foreclosure – that is, a moment when an entire community ceases to express at a symbolic or semantic level any historical questioning, in favour of a delusional spectacularization. Flashing armour and pounding hooves – for them, there is nothing more significant to see. As a hallucination made public spectacle or theatre of blindness, sport replaces for the urban collectivity the effort it would have needed to make to process ongoing historical realities. In terms more political than psychoanalytic, Juvenal denounces the lack of collective responsibility shown by those who pour into the Coliseum in the hope of putting off becoming historically aware.

The well-known expression *panem et circenses*, which has become a cliché,[2] is only one of the references to "circus" among many in Juvenal. More than a single moral transformation, the circus as game reveals in that period a loss of direction. By their lack of responsibility, the oblivious in the stadium are condemned to acts of pure insanity. "When was gambling so reckless? Men come not now with purses to the hazard of the gaming table, but with a treasure-chest beside them. What battles will you there see waged with a cashier for armour-bearer!" (Satire 1, pp. 87–90). It is not only the death of honest trades that the satirist is lamenting – the horn players who tastefully draw the citizens to the municipal arenas – but also intoxication with money beyond all rationality, overseen by the cliques surrounding the temples, ports, and waterways. It is in the circus that the potentates "hold shows of their own, and win applause by slaying whomsoever the mob with a turn of the thumb bids them slay" (Satire 3, pp. 34–37). The spectacle attributes worth unduly to the powerful people who have organized it.

Thus, Juvenal is less saddened to watch the decline of honour than to observe the arbitrary manner in which honours are distributed: "Out of the Knights' stalls, all of you whose means do not satisfy the law. Here let the sons of panders, born in any brothel, take their seats" (Satire 3, pp. 156–157). This hierarchy is based on no particular merit. You can be born in a brothel but demand the best place as soon as you wear clothes that are flamboyant enough to demean anyone showing conspicuous scars.

That circus of appearances has a huge ironic impact: the hidden meaning is the lost child of the literal meaning; throughout the year, a carnival develops in relation to nothing. This is because that game of appearances is based on or refers to no social activity in which one seeks to be absorbed. This forestalls the concerns created by the absence of logic that defines the period. A vicious circle of everything that revolves around the arena, the circus gives its ultimate consistency to a world that is parodied by it:

> Ogulnia hides clothes to see the games; she hires attendants, a litter, cushions, female friends, a nurse, and a fair-haired girl to run her messages; yet she will give all that remains of the family plate, down to the last flagon, to some smooth-faced athlete. Many of these women are poor, but none of them pay any regard to their poverty, or measure themselves by the standard which that prescribes and lays down for them. (Satire 6, pp. 352–359)

The audience of the circus finds in the spectacle a screen against the anxiety they feel in a world that is unravelling precisely because they do not take responsibility for it ... A vicious circle of foreclosure, the coliseum as an institution protects its subjects from a void it is helping generate, in the image of contemporary stadiums rising on suburban sites and opening onto a starry void (see Perelman, 1998; Perelman, 2010).

This exponential disruption of the social bond is observed through the spectacularization of the self in the stands of the coliseum. This shifts the subject from what constitutes its basic historical materiality. The field of visibility of the circus relegates to the invisible the order on the basis of which the link with history was supposed to become possible. The circus anaesthetizes palliatively the psyche against the sufferings brought about by a world that has been turned upside down. Everything is then a matter of will, and of strategy to break the hold of that drug. If in the country you enjoy better, more abundant food, sturdier, bigger houses, considerably reduced risks of assault and fire, then you should not hesitate to go there. "If you can tear yourself away from the games of the Circus" (Satire 3, p. 223), those advantages will be granted to you ... That is the entire question if you want to recover reason to take a rational decision to leave.

When it is too late, when the illusion crumbles and we are overwhelmed by the collapse, the creditors howl and our magnificence vanishes. And still, in forced exile, we still suffer most from the impossibility of attending the games:

> The regular stages are these: money is borrowed in Rome and squandered before the owner's eyes; when some little of it is still left, and the lender's face grows pale, these gentlemen give leg bail, and make off for Baiae and its oyster-beds ... One pang, one sorrow only, afflicts these exiles, that they must, for one season, miss the Circensian games! No drop of blood lingers in their cheek: Shame is ridiculed as she flees from the city, and few would bid her stay. (Satire 11, pp. 52–54)

The expression *bread and circuses*, which history has remembered, resonates here because it reflects the actions of an elite that has strategically distracted the plebeians and other citizens in order to be able to quietly take over the affairs of the world. However, while it is up to the rich to entertain the poor, they are nevertheless dominated themselves by their own spectacle of sport. They are caught up in the carnival as much as anyone, and they organize it to fool themselves. This is suggested, in fact, by the tenth satire, by the exclamation "bread and circuses," which it attributes to the Prefect Sejanus. Juvenal then recounts the tribulations of one of the most influential of the Roman citizens. At a time when rivals were pushing him out of power by spreading false accusations and were about to condemn him to death, that powerful man called for his people's help, but found them powerless because they had been mesmerized by distractions: "And what does the mob of Remus say? It follows fortune, as it always does, and rails against the condemned ... now meddles no more and longs eagerly for just two things – Bread and Games!" (Satire 10, pp. 73–81). We could, of course, read this tirade as an observation on the powerlessness of a people in the face of history, because of diversions that have authority over it. However, in the general spirit of the *Satires*, it is instead a commentary on a pendulum swinging back: the people's unruliness is suddenly harmful to the interests of a leader. The rich are thus seen as responsible for their own misfortune.

> But what grandeur, what high fortune, are worth the having if the joy is overbalanced by the calamities they bring with them? Would you rather choose to wear the bordered robe of the man now being dragged along the streets ... we ask for wife and offspring; but the gods know of what sort the sons, of what sort the wife, will be. Nevertheless that you may have something to pray for, and be able to offer to the shrines entrails and presaging sausages from a white porker, you should pray for a sound mind in a sound body. (Satire 10, pp. 97–99; 354–356)

Morality suggests that the rich who lose themselves in the insanity of the games drag the whole community into an incoherence that puts it in danger.

Through the prism of this favourite quotation from the *Satires*, we have criticized sports in various ways throughout history, whether from a right-wing perspective (i.e., an elite wants to divert the populace in order to put it back to work or induct it into the army), or from a left-wing one (i.e., spectacle and the practice of sport are diversions from revolution). These distinctions are pointless! The *Satires* in any case see in sport the common ground between a community that has lost interest in its traditional responsibilities once people no longer understand what they are and feel overwhelmed, and a ruling class that wants nothing better than to be left to manage alone, to its advantage, the affairs of the common people, even if it is deluding *itself* through its games. Hence this insightful interpretation by Paul Veyne:

> It is posited that the human ideal is that of being an autonomous citizen; every man should do politics and not let the government do it without him. However, men do not conform to this ideal ... Since it is the leaders who benefit most from people being apolitical, aren't they the authors of it? Don't they provide the circus for that? We are taking a gaudy consequence of Augustian depoliticization for a cause (Veyne, 1976, pp. 93–95; translation).

Financial and political leaders enjoy every advantage in agreeing to these sociological arrangements, by offering, sponsoring, and celebrating these popular propensities. Hence the erection of monumental symbols of athletic aesthetics on the plazas of stadiums; hence the endless commentary on "sports events," whose programed nature makes them a series of oxymorons; hence the idea that "The City Is Hockey." To demonstrations of actual athletic performance are added on the stage of sport the murmur of the ideologemes of the time. More than simple entertainment, the theatre of sport features clichés that then become a shared language, one that provides the assurances required by the powerful of the day. Since the end of the nineteenth century and until today, these assurances have related to militarism and eugenics, the spirit of obedience and social Darwinism, nationalism and racism, the cult of performance and the idea of surpassing oneself, individual success and the monetization of success. Always against the backdrop of patriarchy and misogyny.

It is about this spectacle that the common people will feel the most empowered to speak, because their views on it are without consequence for the historical reality for which they no longer seek to take responsibility, since they are so much attuned to it. The social life presented in "the wonderful world of sports" also offers the advantage of requiring a minimal number of prerequisites. In a more and more complex world, and in a political regime in which the pundit now enjoys more credibility than the lawmaker or the court, we find comfort in a sports aesthetic that takes us back to basics. The simplification of the world through the spectacle of sports permits an investment of drives that are not limited to simply screaming in the stands. Quite the contrary, sports make it possible to reflect, extrapolate, express opinions, and debate more than one considers oneself authorized to do when it comes to commenting on the setbacks of the Caisse de dépôt et placement du Québec (Quebec Deposit and Investment Fund), on the extreme domination of subsidized capitalist forces in times of crisis, or on the transformation of Canada into a regulatory paradise for an mining sector that supports sometimes criminal corporations.

Confined as it is to the emptiness of debates that have no real historical consequences, that excess energy has no effect on the ideological regime that organizes these games and gives them a self-interested meaning. We saw the logical conclusion of this in the decision by Prime Minister Stephen Harper to prorogue Canada's parliament in 2010 so that political authorities could invest themselves completely in the propaganda efforts around the Vancouver Olympic Games, exactly as if that high-profile spectacle constituted an affair of state. This catharsis is pernicious: it permits the expression of drives within the framework of a depoliticized public life, but it does not fundamentally achieve in this way an expenditure of energy that would free the community from its internal tensions. On the contrary, the spectacle of sport preserves a repression that goes on and on precisely *because* it consolidates the authority of ideological structures that contribute to the suffering of peoples rather than relieving them of it even temporarily. So we applaud athletes, of whom we say they love their sport while we hate our own work; and we sing the praises of our submission to authority even while feeling that the authority we are subjected to in our own institutions alienates us. Meanwhile, the gods of the stadium are expected to surpass themselves even though they are suffering from the same treatment as us in their professional lives. So it is not out of recklessness that ordinary people, who supposedly have purified their souls by screaming in a stadium, turn their "demonstrations of joy" into riots when their team wins a championship. The spectacle of sports has taught us to express our frustration only behind the false exteriors of the mass sports demonstration:

> You're trained to be obedient; you don't have an interesting job; there's no work around for you that's creative; in the cultural environment you're a passive observer of usually pretty tawdry stuff; political and social life are out of your range, they're in the hands of the rich folk. So what's left? Well, one thing that's left is sports – so you put a lot of the intelligence and the thought and the self-confidence into that. (Chomsky, 2002, p. 99)

Whether or not we read Juvenal as a right-wing reactionary who despises the little people, women, and foreigners, or as a leftist who is passionate about social justice and the defence of collective life, his satires draw attention to the self-interested shedding of responsibility by both leaders and the governed.

"The city is hockey," "L'histoire se joue ici" (History Plays Here), "We are Canadiens," and "Rise together" are advertising slogans without real substance. Through them, the ideological order has occupied public space in Quebec in recent years. This media production offers an "endless loop" of consistency. These slogans calculated by marketing "science" compress the fact of urban reality, as well as the citizens and the history from which they emerge. A francophone population in America that is more lost than ever with respect to the status conferred on it by history finds itself applauding the wealthy of sports show-biz who would themselves have difficulty explaining why they are performing there rather than elsewhere. We need to show this cultural community that it has been reduced to this in its very being. The regime's contradictions are accepted all the better through this aesthetic channel: suffer in the daytime from a lifestyle whose emblems are applauded in the evening. Until the day a crisis comes, sport will fade from the picture to give way to an eruption of public life.

NOTES

1 See the chapter of Jonathan Cha in this book.
2 Historian Paul Veyne's (1976) voluminous study of the Roman world takes its title from the Juvenal quotation.

Conclusion: The Quebecness of the Montreal Canadiens

NICOLAS MOREAU AND
AUDREY LAURIN-LAMOTHE

The winters of my childhood were long, long seasons.
We lived in three places – the school, the church and the skating rink –
but our real life was on the skating rink.

Roch Carrier

The original French version of this book enjoyed extensive media coverage, considering that it was an academic book. We were able to talk with journalists about the relevance of the humanities and social sciences taking an interest in the Montreal Canadiens as a cultural object, in keeping with current trends in cultural studies. The publication of the book in its French version also, interestingly, coincided with an unexpected sports event: the hiring of Randy Cunneyworth as head coach of the Montreal Canadiens. The announcement by the Canadiens' management of the appointment of this unilingual anglophone coach created an explosion of discussion and debate in Quebec society (in specialized and general media, in discussion forums on the Internet, etc.). We were caught up in that whirlwind, in spite of ourselves.

This verbal sparring revolved around two positions: the first, which we could term "romantic," demanded that the coach of Le Grand Club speak both French and English. The reasons given were usually that he would have to talk to many French-language media outlets on a daily basis, that most of the fans were francophones, and that the Canadiens had also been linked to the identity and emancipation of French Canadians. Therefore, hiring a unilingual anglophone coach was an insult to the "History" that linked French Canadians and Le Grand Club. The second position, the "pragmatic" one, favoured hiring the most competent coach possible in order to help Montreal to bring back what had eluded it for too long: the Stanley Cup. A command of the language of Molière should be a secondary consideration.

We could add that issues related to the language(s) spoken by the coach are specific to the Canadiens. The Montreal football team (the Alouettes) does not have to deal with these questions, and neither does the city's soccer team (the Impact). Nor was it an issue for another major franchise in the city, now defunct, the Montreal Expos. These teams can (could) easily hire English-speaking coaches without causing controversy. Good examples of this are the hiring of Tom Higgins in 2014, Dan Hawkins in 2013, and Marc Trestman in 2008 as head coaches of the Alouettes. The media only talked about their CVs and their plans for the team. So it is not necessary for all Montreal sports clubs to maintain a connection with the French fact. Clearly, this is something particular to the Canadiens. The hiring of Michel Therrien as head coach for the 2012–13 season, after Randy Cunneyworth was fired, calmed debate about the language question, since Therrien is a bilingual Quebecer.

Why is the language question so important when it comes to the Canadiens? This can be explained by the fact that hockey is the national winter sport of Canada (which means that qualified candidates who meet the criterion of bilingualism are available, which is possibly less the case for soccer, Canadian football, or baseball). Also, the Habs have a specific history with French Canadians, with Quebecers. Without attempting to rehash the history of Le Grand Club, or of its complex connections with the francophone *and* anglophone communities, the fact is that the Canadiens (and some of the team's players) are often presented socially as a site for the emancipation of French Canadians (see the chapter in this book by Suzanne Laberge). One co-editor of this book, Nicolas Moreau, who is French in origin, recalls that when he immigrated to Quebec, the Canadiens were presented to him as a "social institution," a hybrid team somewhere on a continuum between a city club and a national team. So he began to read up on the subject and watch matches and post-game analyses. A few years later, after he had acquired a better grasp of the club's history, he once started to talk about the quality and impact of a player from the previous decade. He still remembers what a friend said to him: "You're a real Quebecer now, you know the Canadiens."

This should not be understood literally, but rather in the sense that a person who possesses a certain knowledge of the Habs becomes a Quebecer by showing that he or she is interested in a domain that is deeply ingrained in the culture, which suggests that this person has also made efforts to integrate into other spheres of the society. It is also flattering for the Canadiens fan, who is able to validate the importance of the Canadiens as a vector of identity because the other has taken a strong interest in the team. For individuals (new and native-born Canadians) and for cities and nations, sports teams like the Canadiens can constitute vectors for the complex construction and negotiation of identity, which is constantly being redefined.

The Canadiens are key to identity for Montreal and more broadly for Quebec. In this regard, it is interesting to compare them with the Quebec Nordiques. Indeed, this was another question often asked of this book's editors when it came out in French: What would be the impact of a return of the Quebec Nordiques on the Montreal Canadiens? Would the fans who were most concerned about the French fact support the Quebec City team? Would the Canadiens be forced to draft, trade, or sign as free agents more francophone players?

The first thing we would note is that the Nordiques are currently presented as potentially more embedded in the "native soil of Quebec" than the Canadiens. Is this based on the fact that Quebec City is francophone while Montreal is bilingual? Perhaps. In the social construction that is being articulated to promote the return of the Nordiques, people do not hesitate to play up nationalist sentiments. The colour blue (a colour historically associated with Quebec's sovereignty movement), which was also the colour of the jersey of that defunct team, is at the centre of the marketing strategy: the "blue march" that was held on 2 October 2010 to show support for the Nordiques is an excellent example of this. This phenomenon is all the more interesting to explore given that for many political analysts, the defeat of the sovereignty movement in the Quebec referendum of 1995 was attributable in large part to the half-hearted support of inhabitants of Quebec City for the "yes" side.

To get back to the question of the impact of a return of the Nordiques on the Canadiens, it is difficult to give a definitive answer. We *can* say that two players on the 2013 Canadiens were Quebecers (David Desharnais and Francis Bouillon); during the 2014–15 season, there were four (Michaël Bournival, David Desharnais, Gabriel Dumont, Pierre-Alexandre Parenteau). That same season, there were six Quebec players on the Tampa Bay team (Pascal Dupuis, Maxime Lapierre, David Perron, Simon Després, Kristopher Letang, Marc-André Fleury), which also had a francophone president (Mario Lemieux). Meanwhile, the Maple Leafs have two Quebecers in their ranks (Jonathan Bernier,

Stéphane Robidas) but five players from Ontario (David Clarkson, Peter Holland, Joseph Leivo, Nazem Kadri, Daniel Winnik). Note that the last two Leafs head coaches (Randy Carlyle and Peter Horachek) were also from Ontario.

The Canadiens club is still a special case. Its sometimes "romanticized" history is key to its social bond with Montreal and Quebec. Today it serves – perhaps paradoxically, given the romantic vision mentioned above – as one of the ideal-typical bonds between Montreal's francophone and anglophone communities; both identify with "their" Canadiens. Whether it comes to criticizing its performance, its marketing, or its player roster, the fact remains that Quebecers only have one club now, and that club is part of Montreal and of Quebec; it *is* Montreal, it *is* Quebec. Montreal lost its Expos in 2004. The city has never recovered. It would certainly never be the same if the Canadiens ever moved away. Part of the city's DNA would be destroyed.

In conclusion, we would like to thank the University of Toronto Press – in particular, acquisitions editor Douglas Hildebrand for his open-mindedness in giving new life to this book. This proves that while the Canadiens are rooted physically in Montreal and in Quebec, people also care about them in the other provinces of Canada. And it proves, especially, that the fans of the Montreal Canadiens and the fans of the Toronto Maple Leafs can get along.

Bibliography

Aquin, H. and Yanacopoulo, A. (1972). "Éléments pour une phénoménologie du sport." In P. Pagé and R. Legris, eds., *Problèmes d'analyse symbolique* (pp. 115–146). Montreal: Presses de l'Université du Québec.

Ballester, P. (2013). *Fin de cycle. Autopsie d'un système corrompu*. Paris: Éditions de La Martinière.

Bauer, O. (2007)."Vers une communauté d'individus. Le cas de l'Église protestante francophone de Washington, DC." In M. Dumais and J. Richard, *Église et communauté* (pp. 59–78). Montreal: Fides.

Bauer, O. (2009). "Le Canadien est-il une religion?" In O. Bauer and J.-M. Barreau (Eds.), *La religion du Canadien de Montréal* (pp. 64–70). Montreal: Fides.

Bauer, O. (2011). *Une théologie du Canadien de Montréal*. Montreal: Bayard.

Bauer, O., and Barreau, J.-M. (2009). *La religion du Canadien de Montréal*. Montreal: Fides.

Bélanger, A. (2000). "Sports Venues and the Spectacularization of Urban Spaces in North America: The Case of the Molson Center in Montreal." *International Review for the Sociology of Sport*, *35*(3), 399–417.

Bélanger, A., and Nadeau, F. V. (2009). "Entre l'étang gelé et le Centre Bell ... Comment aujourd'hui retricoter le mythe de la Sainte-Famille." In N. Baillargeon and C. Boissimot (Eds.), *La vraie dureté du mental* (pp. 73–93). Quebec City: Les Presses de l'Université Laval.

Bérubé, R. (1973). "Les Québécois, le hockey et le Graal." *Voix et images*, *7*(1), 191–202.

Black, C. (1977). *Duplessis*. Toronto: McClelland and Stewart.

Black, F. (1997). *Habitants et Glorieux: Les Canadiens de 1909 à 1960*. Laval: Éditions Mille-Îles.

Bonneau, L., and Hafsi T. (1996). *Sam Pollock et le Canadien de Montréal: Une gestion du corps et de l'âme*. Sainte-Foy: Presses de l'Université du Québec.

Boivin, P. (2004). Speech to the Board of Trade of Metropolitan Montreal, 24 February. www.ccmm.qc.ca.

Bourdieu, P. (1991). *Language and Symbolic Power*. Trans. G. Raymond and M. Adamson. Cambridge: Polity Press.

Bourque, P. (1996). Quoted in G. Lepore (Ed.). *Le magazine Centre Molson: Match inaugural* Édition spéciale, p. 7.

Brodie, R. (2007). "Vivement la fête chez les amateurs. Un groupe désire organiser des rassemblements après les victoires." *Le Journal de Montréal*, 16 June.

Bromberger, C. (1995). *Le match de football ethnologie d'une passion partisane à Marseille. Naples et Turin.* Paris: Maison des sciences de l'homme.

Buma, M. (2012). *Refereeing Identity: The Cultural Work of Canadian Hockey Novels.* Montreal and Kingston: McGill–Queen's University Press.

Burgener, P. (2006). "Red Mile Opportunity for Community." *Calgary Herald*, 4 May, p. B4.

Bush, G., Sr. (1989). "Remarks at a Briefing on Law Enforcement for United States Attorneys, 1989–06–16." http://www.presidency.ucsb.edu/ws/?pid=17160.

Byrne, R. (2006). *The Secret*. New York: Atria Books.

Canadian Press. (2006). "Sixth NewsWatch." 11 June.

Canadiens Hockey Club. (1996). "Forum." Publicity document.

Carrier, R. (1984). *The Hockey Sweater.* Trans. S. Fischman. Toronto: Tundra Books.

Castel, R., and Haroche, C. (2001). *Propriété privée, propriété sociale, propriété de soi: Entretiens sur la construction de l'individu moderne*. Paris: Fayard.

Champagne, S. (2010). "Le Canadien dans la toponymie québécoise." *La Presse*, 14 January.

Chomsky, N. (2002). *Understanding Power: The Indispensable Chomsky.* New York: The New Press.

Clément, É. (2008). "La Sainte-Flanelle aura son avenue." *La Presse*, 5 December.

Cyr, L., and Leblanc. C. (1999). *Mon frère Richard.* Ad Hoc films.

Daigneault, D. (2008). "La Place du Centenaire. Un site à visiter absolument." *Le magazine officiel de la Place du Centenaire*, p. 8.

Deachman, B. (2007). "Welcome to 'Hockey Town.'" *Ottawa Citizen*, 20 May, p. A3.

Derworiz, C. (2005). "Council Seeks Balance on Red Mile: Aldermen Will Debate Proposal for 17th Avenue." *Calgary Herald*, 29 November, p. B7.

Desaulniers, D. (2007). "'I'm So Fantastically, Unbelievably Happy': Fistpumping, Flag-waving Fans Pour into the Streets to Celebrate the Sens." *Ottawa Citizen*, 20 May, p. D6.

Desrosiers, P., and Thibault, S. (2009). *Les francs-tireurs.* Émission 286, Télé-Québec. February.

Du Gay, P. (1997). "Introduction." In P. Du Gay (Ed.), *Production of Culture/Cultures of Production* (pp. 1–6). London: Open University and Sage Publications.

Duperreault, J. R. (1981). "L'affaire Richard: A situational analysis of the Montreal Hockey Riot of 1955." *Canadian Journal of Sport History, 12*(1), 66–83.

Durkheim, Émile. *The Rules of Sociological Method.* Trans. W. D. Halls. New York: The Free Press, 1982.

Eckler, R. (2004). "A Whole Lotta Love on Calgary's Red Mile." *National Post*, 31 May, p. A1.

Ehrenberg, A. (1991). *Le culte de la performance.* Paris: Hachette Littératures.

Ehrenberg, A. (1998). *La fatigue d'être soi: Dépression et société.* Paris: Odile Jacob.

Ehrenreich, B. (2005). *Bait and Switch: The (Futile) Pursuit of the American Dream.* New York: Metropolitan Books.

Fecteau, J.-M. (1998). "Lendemains de défaite: les Rébellions comme histoire et mémoire." *Bulletin d'histoire politique, 7*(1), 19–28.

Fischler, S., and Richard, M. (1971). *Les Canadiens sont là! La plus grande dynastie du hockey*. Toronto: Prentice-Hall.

Fisher, Red. (2007). "Thousands of Empty Seats in Hockeytown a Direct Result of Overpriced Playoff Tickets." *The Gazette*, 28 April.

Fleuriel, S., and Schotté, M. (2008). *Sportifs en danger. La condition des travailleurs sportifs*. Broissieux: Éditions du croquant.

Fortney, V. (2006). "Inside the Oil Slick: It May Not Be the Red Mile, but This Is the Place to Be." *Calgary Herald*, 12 May, p. A3.

Frei, T. (2006). "Qu'est-ce qu'une ville de hockey?" http://www.rds.ca/hockey, 1 September.

Garand, M.-È. (2009). "Le Canadien de Montréal est-il une religion ou la religion des Canadiens?" Paper presented to the conference "The Habs Religion," Montreal, 16 January.

Gauthier, R., and Bisson, P.-R. (1990). *L'architecture de Montréal.* Montreal: Libre Expression.

Goyens, C., Turowetz, A., and Dugay, J.-L., (1996). *The Montreal Forum: Forever Proud.* Westmount: Effix.

Grossberg, L. (1992). "Mapping Popular Culture." In L. Grossberg, *We Gotta Get Out of This Place: Popular Conservatism and Postmodern Culture* (pp. 69–88). London: Routledge.

Gruneau, R., and Whitson, D. (1993). *Hockey Night in Canada. Sport, Identities, and Cultural Politics.* Toronto: Garamond Press.

Gruneau, R., and Whitson, D. (2006). *Artificial Ice: Hockey, Culture, and Commerce*. Toronto: Garamond Press.

Guay, D. (1990). *L'histoire du Hockey au Québec: Origine et développement d'un phénomène culturel*. Montreal: Éditions JCL.

Hall, S. (1997). *Representation: Cultural Representations and Signifying Practices*. London: Open University/Sage Publications.

Hall, S. (2005). "Notes on Deconstructing 'The Popular.'" In R. Guins and O. Z. Cruz (Eds.), *Popular Culture: A Reader* (pp. 64–71). London: Sage Publications.

Harvey, J. (2006). "Whose Sweater Is This? The Changing Meaning of Hockey in Quebec." In R. Gruneau and D. Whitson (Eds.). *Artificial Ice: Hockey, Culture, and Commerce* (pp. 29–52). Toronto: Garamond Press.

Herrmann, M. (2007). "Hockey Fever Breaks Out All over Buffalo." *Buffalo News*, 29 April, p. B6.

Higgins, M. (2007). "Another Hockeytown." *New York Times*, 4 May, p. 6.

Holman, A. C. (Ed.) (2009). *Canada's Game: Hockey and Identity*. Montreal and Kingston: McGill–Queen's University Press.

Hynes, J., and Smith, G. (2008). *Saving Face: The Art and History of the Goalie Mask*. Mississauga: Wiley.

Juvenal. *The Satires*. Trans. G.G. Ramsay. New York: G. G. Putnam and Sons, 1918.

Katz, S. (1955). "Strange Forces Behind the Richard Hockey Riot," *Maclean's*, 17 September, 68.

Klein, N. (2000). *No Logo: Taking Aim at the Brand Bullies*. Toronto: Vintage Canada.

Lafleur, G. (2008). "Une victoire entachée." *Le Journal de Montréal*, 26 April, p. 106.

Lasorsa, S. (2011). *La rivalité Canadien-Nordiques*. Quebec City: Presses de L'Université Laval.

Laurin-Lamothe, A. (2011). "L'investissement subjectif des travailleurs: contribution à la sociologie critique du management." Master's thesis, Université du Québec à Montréal, Sociology Department.

Laurin-Lamothe, A., and Moreau, N. (2011). *Le Canadien de Montréal: Une légende repensée*. Montreal: Presses de L'Université de Montréal.

Lavoie, M. (1997a). *Avantage Numérique: L'argent et la ligue nationale de Hockey*. Hull: Éditions Vents d'Ouest.

Lavoie, M. (1997b). *Désavantage numérique: Les Francophones dans la LNH*. Hull: Éditions Vents d'Ouest.

Leipsic, B. J. (2004). "Go Jets, go!" *National Post*, 31 March, p. A19.

Lyotard, J.-F. (1984). *The Postmodern Condition: A Report on Knowledge.* Paris: Éditions de Minuit.

Macafee, M., Canadian Press, (2006). "Game 1 Loss Leads to Quiet Night on Edmonton's Trendy Whyte Avenue," 6 June.

Maniago, S. (2007). "A Call to Action – Believe in Blue." *Canucks.com,* 28 April.

Marois, M. (1993). "Sport, politique et violence: une interprétation de la violence des foules aux événements sportifs et de la médiatisation de cette violence." PhD diss., Université de Montréal.

Marr, N., and Spivak, W. (2005). "100 Years of History." *Calgary Herald,* 1 September, p. A15.

Mason, D. (2006). "Expanding the Footprint." In R. Gruneau and D. Whitson (Eds.), *Artificial Ice: Hockey, Culture, and Commerce* (pp. 181–199). Toronto: Garamond Press.

Mathieu, A. (2009). "Inauguration de l'avenue des Canadiens-de-Montréal." *La Presse,* 9 October.

Mauss, M. (1966). *The Gift: Forms and Functions of Exchange in Archaic Societies.* London: Cohen and West.

McKinley, M. (2000). *Putting a Roof on Winter: Hockey's Rise from Sport to Spectacle.* Vancouver: Greystone.

McKinley, M. (2006). *Hockey: A People's History.* Toronto: McClelland and Stewart.

Melançon, B. (2006). *Les yeux de Maurice Richard: Une histoire culturelle.* Montreal: Fides.

Melançon, B. (2008). "Chanter les Canadiens." Paper presented to the conference "100 ans de polysémie. Regards et réflexions sur les Canadiens de Montréal." 77e Congrès de l'ACFAS, Ottawa, 15 May.

Molson, E. (1996). Quoted in C. Goyens, A. Turowetz, and J.-L. Duguay. *Le Forum de Montréal. La fierté pour toujours. 1924–1996.* Westmount: Les Éditions Effix.

Moreau, N. (2008). "Histoire de la dialectique sport / société et évolution des formes de racisme aux États-Unis: le cas des Afro-américains." *Esprit critique, 11*(2), p. 18.

Moreau, N. (2009). *État dépressif et temporalité: Contribution à la sociologie de la santé mentale.* Montréal: Liber.

Morley D., and Chen K.-H. (Eds.). (1996). *Stuart Hall: Critical Dialogues in Cultural Studies.* London: Routledge.

Müller, D. (2008). *Le football, ses dieux et ses démons: Menaces et atouts d'un jeu déréglé.* Geneva and Montreal: Labor et Fides.

Myers, S. (2006). "Planners Share Vision of 'People's' Red Mile." *Calgary Herald*, 11 January, p. B5.

O'Brien, A. (1961). *Rocket Richard*. Toronto: Ryerson Press.

Ottawa Sun. (2007). "Shooting for Mile High: Fans Invited to Elgin St. Playoff Party Zone." 16 June.

Pellerin, J.-M. (1998). *Maurice Richard, l'idole d'un peuple*. Montreal: Trustar.

Perelman, M. (1998). *Le stade barbare*. Paris: Mille et une nuits.

Perelman, M. (2010). *L'ère des stades: Genèse et structure d'un espace historique*. Paris: Infolio.

Pinard, R. (2000). *La révolution du travail. De l'artisan au manager*. Montreal: Liber.

Pronkin, A. (2009). "Les œuvres caritatives du Canadien, là où l'esprit circule!" In O. Bauer and J.-M. Barreau (Eds.), *La religion du Canadien de Montréal* (pp. 139–158). Montreal: Fides.

Prunier, J. (2007). Marketing Department of the Canadiens Hockey Club, 12 January. Telephone conversation.

Public Policy Forum. (1999). *The National Hockey League in Canada*. Ottawa: Industry Canada.

Queval, I. (2004). *S'accomplir ou se dépasser: essais sur le sport contemporain*. Paris: Gallimard.

Radio-Canada. (2012). "La place du Centenaire démantelée," 16 July. http://ici.radio-canada.ca/sports/hockey/2012/07/16/002-lnh-canadien-construction.shtml.

Raymond, B. (2006). "La rue Maurice-Richard? Si le Rocket revenait au Centre Bell ..." *Le Journal de Montréal*, 7 December.

Richelieu, A. 2003. "Mon équipe est une marque." Working document. Faculté des sciences de l'administration, Université Laval.

Rioux, B. (2012). "La Place du Centenaire survivra." 16 July, QMI Agency, http://fr.canoe.ca/sports/nouvelles/hockey/canadiens/archives/2012/07/20120716-122132.html.

Robidoux. M. A. (2001). *Men at Play: A Working Understanding of Professional Hockey*. Montreal and Kingston: McGill–Queen's University Press.

Rowe, D., J. Mckay, and T. Miller. (2000). "Come Together: Sport, Nationalism, and the Media Image." In L. A. Wenner (Ed.), *Media Sport* (pp. 119–133). London: Routledge.

Sadava, M. (2007). "Sens Fever Brings Back Memories of Oilers Run: But So Far Capital Crowds Are Having Peaceful Fun." *Edmonton Journal*, 26 May, p. B3.

Sennett, R. (1977). *The Fall of Public Man*. New York: Knopf .

Sennett, R. (1998). *The Corrosion of Character: The Personal Consequences of Work in the New Capitalism*. New York: W.W. Norton.

Sharp, D. (2006). *National Post* (*Detroit Free Press*), 7 October, p. FW9.

Sinclair-Faulkner, T. (2005). "A Puckish Reflection on Religion in Canada." In J. L. Price (Ed.), *From Season to Season: Sports as American Religion* (pp. 185–202). Macon: Mercer University Press.

Slack, J. D. (1996). "The Theory and Method of Articulation in Cultural Studies." In S. Hall, D. Morley and K.-H. Chen (Eds.) *Stuart Hall: Critical Dialogues in Cultural Studies* (pp. 112–130). London: Routledge.

Storey, J. (2001). "What Is Popular Culture?" In *Cultural Theory and Popular Culture: An Introduction* (pp. 1–16). Essex: Pearson.

Taylor, S. (2004). "Tampa' s 'White Out' Pales Next to Original Original." *Winnipeg Free Press*, 4 June, p. C3.

Thomazeau, F. (2014). *L'imposture du sport*. Paris: Éditions First.

Trudel, P. (2001). Preface in McKinley, M. *Un toit pour le hockey*. Montreal, Hurtubise.

Van der Leeuw, G. *Religion in Essence and Manifestation: A Study in Phenomenology*. Trans. J. E. Turner. New York: Macmillan, 1938.

Veyne, P. (1976). *Le pain et le cirque: Sociologie historique d'un pluralisme politique*. Paris: Seuil.

Wacquant, L. (2004). *Punir les pauvres: le nouveau gouvernement de l'insécurité sociale*. Marseille: Agone.

Wigge, L. (2002). *NHL Sporting News*, 7 January.

Wind, H. W. (1954). "Fire on the Ice." *Sports Illustrated*, 6 December.

Wong, J.-C. (2005). *Lords of the Rinks: The Emergence of the National Hockey League, 1875–1936*. Toronto: University of Toronto Press.

Wong, J.-C. (Ed.) (2009). *Coast to Coast: Hockey in Canada to the Second World War*. Toronto: University of Toronto Press.

Yonnet, P. (1998). *Système des sports*. Paris: Gallimard.

Contributors

Olivier Bauer was born in Switzerland. His professional life has spanned three continents – in France, Switzerland, Tahiti, and Washington – as a minister in various Protestant churches, and as a teaching assistant and lecturer in universities in Neuchâtel and Lausanne. Since 2005, he has been a professor in the Faculty of Theology and Religious Sciences at the Université de Montréal. His research is on the transmission of faith through the six senses, on the spiritual value of food, and on the relationship between sports and religion. On these themes, he has a blog called "Une théologie au quotidien [theology in daily life]: olivierbauer.org.

Jonathan Cha is an urbanologist and landscape architect. He teaches at the School of Landscape Architecture of the Faculty of Planning at the Université de Montréal and at the UQAM School of Design. His studies and professional duties are related to analysis of heritage and the characterization of urban and landscape forms in public places and urban spaces. He has completed a PhD at the Université du Québec à Montréal and at the Institut national de la recherche scientifique in urbanization, culture, and society, in collaboration with the Institut d'urbanisme de Paris of the Université Paris-Est.

Alain Deneault is the author of *Imperial Canada Inc.: Legal Haven of Choice for the World's Mining Industries* (Talonbooks, 2012), *Offshore Tax Havens and the Rule of Global Crime* (The New Press, 2011), and *Paul Martin & Companies: Sixty Theses on the Alegal Nature of Tax Havens* (Talonbooks, 2006). In 2009 he taught a course on the sociology and aesthetics of the mass spectacle of sports in the sociology department of the Université du Québec à Montréal.

Suzanne Laberge has a PhD in anthropology and an MA in kinesiology from the Université de Montréal; she is a professor in the kinesiology department of the Université de Montréal. Her research deals with various questions related to the relationship between sports and society, such as the construction of masculinity and femininity in the practice of sports, the social dimensions and ethics of doping, the economic cost of elite sports, and the use of sports as a way to prevent juvenile delinquency and to keep kids in school.

Audrey Laurin-Lamothe is pursuing a PhD in sociology at UQAM on the theme of economic elites. Her research activities deal with hockey, management, corporations, subjectivity, and work, and are part of the work of the Collectif d'analyse sur la financiarisation du capitalisme avancé (CAFCA) (Collective for the Analysis of the Financialization of Advanced Capitalism), affiliated with the Canada Research Chair in Globalization, Citizenship, and Democracy.

Nicolas Moreau is an associate professor in the School of Social Work at the University of Ottawa and has a PhD in sociology. He is interested in the connections between mental health problems and social norms in contemporary Western societies, and in sport as a tool for psychosocial development and as a normative laboratory of the social world.

Chloé Nahas has an MA in social work from the University of Ottawa and is very interested in hockey as a social phenomenon. Her area of interest is social normativity and the impact of current social norms on the living conditions of Aboriginal women.

Marie-Pier Rivest is a PhD candidate and part-time professor at the University of Ottawa's School of Social Work. Her research interests include social work interventions in mental health, the concept of empowerment, and the critical study of contemporary social normativity.

Fannie Valois-Nadeau is a PhD candidate in communications at the Université de Montréal. After writing a sociology thesis at UQAM in which she analysed discussion forums on the Montreal Canadiens, she is working on the practices of memory that emerged around the centenary of the team. Her main research subjects are the concepts of memory, tradition, heritage, and popular culture.